CAN I GO & PLAY NOW?

Rethinking the Early Years

GREG BOTTRILL

SAGE

Los Angeles | London | New Delhi
Singapore | Washington DC | Melbourne

Los Angeles | London | New Delhi
Singapore | Washington DC | Melbourne

SAGE Publications Ltd
1 Oliver's Yard
55 City Road
London EC1Y 1SP

SAGE Publications Inc.
2455 Teller Road
Thousand Oaks, California 91320

SAGE Publications India Pvt Ltd
B 1/I 1 Mohan Cooperative Industrial Area
Mathura Road
New Delhi 110 044

SAGE Publications Asia-Pacific Pte Ltd
3 Church Street
#10-04 Samsung Hub
Singapore 049483

Editor: Amy Thornton
Production Editor: Chris Marke
Marketing Manager: Lorna Patkai
Cover design: Wendy Scott
Typeset by: C&M Digitals (P) Ltd, Chennai, India
Printed in the UK

First published in 2018 by Learning Matters Ltd

Library of Congress Control Number: 2017961767

British Library Cataloguing in Publication Data

A catalogue record for this book is available from
the British Library

ISBN 978-1-5264-2327-6 (pbk)
ISBN 978-1-5264-2326-9

At SAGE we take sustainability seriously. Most of our products are printed in the UK using FSC papers and boards.
When we print overseas we ensure sustainable papers are used as measured by the PREPS grading system.
We undertake an annual audit to monitor our sustainability.

CONTENTS

ABOUT THE AUTHOR

An experienced Early Years teacher, Greg is passionate about real play, the magic of childhood and putting children at the heart of their learning adventure.

Inspired by theorists such as Loris Malaguzzi, EY consultant Alistair Bryce-Clegg and family psychologist Steve Biddulph among others, he is committed to making a positive change to children's experience in society and education. He makes no claim to be right about everything, but hopes that this book will at least enable you to undertake your own journey of discovery that will lead to better, brighter things.

He lives with his family, two cats and Bonnie the dog in the Mid-Devon countryside.

This book is dedicated to the greatest team that ever lived and you, wherever you may go and whoever you may become – it's the little things...

INTRODUCTION

Education is entwined with society; it runs like a thread through it. In the adult world we think that the children we shape today become the adults of tomorrow, so we put great efforts and considerable public money into doing so. The adult world looks for outcomes for this investment. It looks to business leaders and corporations and in doing so devises a system of grading and measurement that can serve these sectors. In turn, we then put great pressure on our schools and teachers to create these children of tomorrow. League tables, phonics screening tests, SATs, GCSEs, a chain of hoops to jump through and of inadvertent pressure on our young people today. We seem obsessed with grading, passing and failing, being good enough or not good enough.

In doing so we are rushing headlong into forming a society that is low on self-esteem, high on ill-health and 'spiritually' impoverished. We have a teaching sector in which recruitment is becoming increasingly difficult, where morale is low and new teacher retention lasts on average around five years. It's a bleak picture.

Perhaps if you are reading this as a trainee teacher, you might be thinking that all is lost and to pack up your things, and go and search for an alternative career. Yet teaching is a wonderful occupation. Like all jobs, it has its highs and lows, its challenges and pressures, but there is nothing better than seeing children in your care thrive and flourish. An adventure with young people is the best kind and in Early Years you have the opportunity to go on an adventure of a lifetime. My hope is that by the end of this book, you will know that the adventure is possible and that the key to unlocking it lies in your very own hands.

Our map for the journey ahead begins with looking at the child and how they are and need to be right at the centre of their learning. It then takes us to explore the importance of understanding children's next steps and how the environment we create through our continuous provision needs to lie at the heart of our Early Years practice. There will be challenges along the way and nagging doubts that are an inevitable part of change, but all the time, as we are reading, we need to hold on to the basic acceptance that children need the space to be themselves for their own growth, and that this can only truly happen if we enable play – play that is from the child.

We'll confront the adult world and its demands of the child and how it attempts to stifle children's 'language', and the need for us to be facilitators rather than teachers. Then it's headlong into the 3Ms, the approach that has the ability to meet the adult world's predilection for data, measurability and progress while at the same time creating the conditions for children to engage in joyful, collaborative play – this, I hope, is the exciting bit. What follows directly after this I'll keep a secret for now, but I don't think you'll be disappointed. Then it will be time to explore the great outdoors and last, but not least, we'll find time to consider the adults around us in the adult world and how we can utilise or shape them for the benefit of our children.

I guess there's no better time than now to explain the book's title. I'm sure you've heard it in the classroom from children, who after sitting at your table with you filling out some worksheet or other, or while you try to get children to do what you've asked them to do on your planning sheet with spongy letters in the water tray, will say in a pained tone: 'Can I go and play now?'

Just hearing those six words should be enough to tell you that your practice possibly needs to change. It's a product of boredom, disengagement, of unplayful Not-Play. Once you get to the end of this book and if you feel inspired to try the approach outlined in its pages, I'm convinced that you'll never hear those six words again.

Happy reading and happy playing, Greg :)

PART 1

WHERE DO WE GO FROM HERE?

CHAPTER 1

THE CHILD AT THE CENTRE OF THE UNIVERSE

'A broken heart is a brilliant start ... ' – The Mary Onettes

The world of education is an amazing and rewarding world to be in, but there is a sense among many that work within it that there is something not quite right, that all is not well. Every teacher and educator has a concept of what education is and what it isn't. Many would want to change education, many have tried, few have succeeded. Education policy is something that seems to be inflicted on teachers in the twenty-first century – it doesn't feel collaborative and it often feels that no one is listening to common sense.

When I told my father that I was going to train to be a primary teacher, his first words, as someone who had spent his entire life as a teacher and latterly as a teacher-trainer, were: 'Don't – it's not what you think it is ...' And how right he was. I seemed to have entered a universe where stress, pressure, constant change, moving of goalposts, learning walks, display monitoring, data collections and performance management have slowly wrung out the pleasures that made teaching a career to be proud of.

'From revolution to revelation ...' – My October Symphony, *Pet Shop Boys*

Trying to fix something is never straightforward. Sometimes the answer lies outside our normal day-to-day experiences or it needs someone to point us in the right direction. Last year, before going on a family holiday in Cornwall, I recognised that I was in a phase of my life that I knew I needed to change. The problem was that I didn't know where to turn. I would go on long dog walks and wrestle in my brain, sit by the fire with a bottle of red and ponder or throw myself into social situations just to distract my brain. And then, almost out of the blue a good friend mentioned a book in passing that she had heard about and how it might be worth a read. That book was *The Rhythm of Life* by Matthew Kelly (not he of *Stars in Their Eyes* fame) and over the course of the family holiday within the space of four days, having read it cover to cover, my whole life changed (Kelly M [2002] *The Rhythm Of Life*, Crowborough: Beacon Publishing).

I realised that I was enduring an internal struggle with my life and its significance. I was toiling in an education system that seemed detached and beyond my control. I knew that I wanted to change this somehow but couldn't find the internal dialogue to begin this process. But there, staring back at me from *The Rhythm of Life* lay the answer:

> *Lasting happiness and fulfilment are not the by-products of doing and having ... Who you become is infinitely more important than what you do or what you have. The meaning and purpose of life is for you to become the best-version-of-yourself ...*

> (p. 29)

> *To be what we are, and to become what we are capable of becoming, is the only end in life.*

> (Robert Louis Stevenson, p. 30)

And, perhaps most tellingly of all, his view of education:

> *We teach more and more about less and less. We don't draw out the individual. We impose upon the individual – systems and structures. We don't reverence individuality, we don't treasure it, we stifle it ... we don't educate, we formulate. We abandon the individual in his or her need and uniqueness and 'impose' the same upon all.*

> (p. 105)

And so therein lies the challenge: if we know or even suspect that there needs to be a change, why don't we become the change we want to see? How can we, as educators, become the best-version-of-ourselves – not just in our own selves but also within our classrooms, our interactions with colleagues and in the positive energy giving that we can bring every day with us through the school gates? And that is the change that I want to become.

I want to change our view of Early Years and our very practice

I want to change, not just through this book but through my life, my example, through my dialogues with parents and colleagues. Some may see me as a bald-headed beardy man in his mid-40s on some crusade, but if my voice is joined by your voice and your voice is joined by another, and so on and on, can we not begin to orchestrate change that we want to see and truly become the teachers that we want to be? And maybe that's a dilly-daydream, but wouldn't it be better to die trying than just roll over and accept a system and structure that deep down in our hearts we know to be broken and no longer fit for purpose?

I Am the Cosmos, I Am the Wind – *Chris Bell, Big Star*

Increasingly, or so it would seem, mainstream education is fast becoming something that is done to a child – an act of imposition: we teach, children learn. The adult imparts their wisdom, their light, their understanding so that the child can receive and fill themselves up from top to toe. It's as though children are empty pots on a factory floor advancing along a chain at various stages being topped up along the way. And this is how a modern-day education system would want you to think – to buy into a system that enables grading and measuring, that produces data that in turn allows it to grade a school, which in turn enables it to grade itself. It's like the brainchild of an Orwellian dystopia which, left unchallenged, will continue to use education as a self-serving entity. It puts the individual child out of the frame at the expense of focusing on itself.

Shamefully, perhaps, this data-led measured-based approach is bleeding into Early Years and not only creating a system that seems to look past the child-as-the-child, but ultimately misses the very obvious point that when we work with young children we are dealing with people not numbers, with development not progress, and with what should be joy not mechanical learning by rote. Our leaders appear to be fixated with the 'success' of Far East education systems that enable measurability to the nth degree, ignoring our children's need for energy, their true creativity, their real sense of who they are.

Now, this book isn't going to be a call to arms or a rallying cry to rush the Houses of Parliament, a baying crowd with pitchforks waving, flags fluttering in the breeze. It is, however, going to show you that there is a way to work within the system that will give you the outcomes that, as an adult, you are expected to achieve, while at the same time giving your children wonderful and enriching experiences that will both enable them and nurture their own 'soulness'. And if you discover the success of this approach, why not then tell someone else, who will tell someone else, and so on? Lo and behold, we have our revelation *and* a revolution.

What is required for this approach to be successful?

A simple word: faith. Faith in yourself, faith in your innate sense of what education really should be and, most importantly, faith in children.

Perhaps it would help if we focused on arguably one of Europe's finest educational minds, Loris Malaguzzi, to enable us to switch our focus from outcome-driven and on to a child-driven pedagogy. Malaguzzi was a man who had real faith in young children – he saw them as citizens, as people who participated, who had thoughts, actions, dreams, imagination, all of which lie beyond the interpretation of the adult world. Emerging as a society from the aftermath of the Second World War, he began to set about defining an approach that would create a society that valued children and their education. He had a vision that children could be enabled to realise and express their own ideas along the principles of respect, responsibility and community, and could do so through being empowered to explore and discover via a curriculum that was essentially self-created and travelled through with the gentle and helping hands of adults.

His poem *The Hundred Languages of Children* beautifully sums up his vision of children, and I would challenge you to disagree with any of its sentiments:

The child
is made of one hundred.
The child has
a hundred languages
a hundred hands
a hundred thoughts
a hundred ways of thinking
of playing, of speaking.
A hundred always a hundred
ways of listening
of marveling, of loving
a hundred joys
for singing and understanding
a hundred worlds
to discover
a hundred worlds

to invent

a hundred worlds

to dream.

The child has

a hundred languages

(and a hundred hundred hundred more)

but they steal ninety-nine.

The school and the culture

separate the head from the body.

They tell the child:

to think without hands

to do without head

to listen and not to speak

to understand without joy

to love and to marvel

only at Easter and at Christmas.

They tell the child:

to discover the world already there

and of the hundred

they steal ninety-nine.

They tell the child:

that work and play

reality and fantasy

science and imagination

sky and earth

reason and dream

are things

that do not belong together.

And thus they tell the child

that the hundred is not there.

The child says:

No way. The hundred is there.

How true and how damning. The adult world seems perennially to want children to be seen and not heard, but the hundred is there in spite of this. We hear the hundred every day. Children want you to hear their joy, their representations of the world, their understanding, their delight, their inquisitiveness. Unfortunately, we are often guilty of not listening; of not taking heed; of not paying attention; of only truly having brain space for our own planned activity, our own impositions, our own pressures. And children soon learn that you aren't listening. They soon discover that the adult world is detached from theirs, that they have to do what you want them to do, to jump through the hoop, to follow-the-leader, to tiptoe through the bluebells. Children's marvel, their desire to invent and their dreams are nothing if they are denied the opportunity to be.

If only we could find a way to listen ...

If only we had enough faith ... enough faith to not steal ninety-nine, enough faith to agree with children that the hundred is there. Enough faith to be on their side for once, to think like the child that you once were and to see the world through their eyes. Isn't that what we want our children to do: marvel, dream, laugh, sing, love, think?

It all seems so glaringly obvious. I don't think anyone in their right mind would deny that those things aren't the cornerstones of what children should experience. But how many days within the school system does this truly happen for children? The block to all this is, of course, the adult world. The world that we alluded to at the beginning of this chapter: measuring, analysing, rapid progress, closing the gap, data outcomes, performance. None of these things matter to children – they are too in the moment, too joyfully oblivious. So, it is the adult world that is drowning out their voice, telling children that the hundred is not there. It is the adult world that denies the marvel, the dream, the love, the thought.

Now we as adults can't just walk away from the adult world and its pressures, and arguably we have a duty to work within the system that we have. We can't just pretend that it doesn't exist – after all, your performance management relies on the outcomes of the adult world and without these, dear reader, you would most likely find yourself out of work. So there needs to be a way that both worlds can meet, and happily there is. Your passport to this approach relies on you to feel deep down that children have a voice and to be open to hearing it.

You as a practitioner need to have an ingrained sense of what it is that children truly need

Children don't need adults who are only there because they didn't know what else to do in life; they don't need adults who are only there because they see themselves on a career ladder; they don't need adults who merely have good intentions; and they certainly don't need adults who can only think like an adult. Children need you to listen, to watch, to participate – you as an adult literally need *to get down with the kids*.

You cannot access the real world of children if you cannot or are unwilling to do this. All too often we see teachers entering the profession with personal ambition or with the lack of integrity to stop for one moment and question or challenge what it is we are doing with children day in and day out. Increasingly, the obsession with MATs and Ofsted-driven outcomes blinds us as adults – we are being led on a merry dance by a piper who calls the tune but is somehow playing a broken pipe. The blanket approach based on accountability and outcomes completely misses the true and richer nature of childhood, of child development. It closes its ears to the child's voice and instead blah-blahs over the top of it until it is drowned out. The child has to be at the centre of our thinking, of our nurturing, and for this to truly happen then we must put meta-phorical masking tape over our mouths, prick up our ears and listen.

Education needs people who have pedagogy at the heart of their desire to be a teacher

Your own personal belief is vital for you to be a truly effective practitioner. Too often we see schools that are driven by a hunger for data outcomes and not by the children's best interests or personal development.

Early Years must resist the top-down mentality of seeing children as product and as outcome. Early Years holds the key to successful child development. However, nine times out of ten we see the immediate close-down of this in its truest sense once children arrive in the Year 1 classroom. It takes a brave heart and mind of school leadership to see children being truly enabled in Key Stage 1. School is and has always been a top-down pyramid where Year 6 and often the Year 6 teacher's attitudes filter down. This often leads to children being compartmental-ised, boxed up and factory-ised because leadership doesn't understand Early Years. It is frequently the case that a general teaching degree places very little emphasis on Early Years. There's a perception that Early Years isn't 'proper' teaching.

This immediately creates a barrier between the worlds of Key Stage 2/Key Stage 1 and Early Years. Early Years somehow becomes something different and other worldly. It transfers itself unfortunately into the workplace once students become teachers. All too often teachers say, 'Well, it's just Early Years, they soon grow out of it, play isn't learning, they'll start proper school in Year 1.'

The tragedy of this is that it gets passed on to parents who then begin to see Year 1 as proper school or where their children begin to learn. This has a huge impact on how Early Years is perceived. What needs to occur is a revelation that Early Years and its practice is *the* most important time of a child's school life and one in which they will do their crucial learning. By 'learning' I mean their perception of what school is, what teachers are and, most importantly, who they, as children, are and what they can achieve. Since we are seemingly hell bent on grading, classifying, assessing, judging and measuring children, it would perhaps seem that there is a picture of a somewhat hopeless cause. This is far from the truth – as Early Years practitioners we need to begin to make our voices heard.

'We wanna be free, we wanna be free to do what we wanna do ... we wanna have a good time and that's what we're going to do!' – The Wild Angels (1966)

If freedom comes from listening to children's voices, then we have to prepare ourselves to listen. We have to create the conditions for children to be heard. We need to fashion the space within our own adult minds to ensure that this can happen. In short, we need to let go.

If our children are really to have their voices heard, then we need to ensure that we are not blocking the airwaves with what we perceive to be their best interests, with what we want or need them to learn.

Your adult voice cannot be their voice

With the best will in the world, your half-termly themes such Spring, Chinese New Year, People Who Help Us, Under The Sea, Dinosaurs, and so on are not the children's voice – they are yours. Nowhere in the EYFS does it say that these topics are what needs teaching, yet we find them in many Reception classes being taught year in and year out. But have the children expressed a desire to find out about these things? Have they ever once talked about or demonstrated how they would love to explore the role of the dentist to the extent that every bit of the continuous provision resembles a dental practice with a neat and tidy People Who Help Us display? I'm not denying that some of these themes contain within them some important messages, but I would equally argue that it doesn't need often tenuous links to a theme because the adults have it in their planning and have had it in their planning since three years ago.

Thematic approaches are adult-led without a doubt – they drown out the child's interests, look beyond them through a fug of 'planned activity' and prescribed outcome. A child-led approach is wild and free, it roams from minute to minute, hour to hour, day to day, sometimes veering off, sometimes simple, sometimes brilliant, sometimes soaring, often taking you to places you could never imagine: always exciting, always something different, forever changing, never standing still. Always, always beautiful.

'Don't be afraid of yourself ...' Old Coast Road, *The Church*

So on one side we have the child's world and on the other the adult's. How to make the two come together, how to meet the needs and rights of the child to explore and discover while at the same time meeting our own adult needs for measurable progress and outcome? By itself, the beauty of children's natural desire to interpret and express their world could quite happily exist without the influence of the adult world, but the need for data and accountability demands adult influence. The Senior Leadership Team demands an outcome.

In Early Years, the 'goal' is for the maximum number of children within your class to make Early Learning goals or above. It's the crude measuring stick for both the child's and your success. It's the per cent that keeps you awake at night and makes you reach for that second glass of red on a Tuesday evening. The subsequent chapters of this book are going to show you just how to achieve this while balancing the need for children to be free, happy and childlike. Before we get to those chapters, we need to make sure that in our minds two things are clear: skills-focused learning and children's Next Steps. Without these two central tenets you will never achieve your adult-led outcomes. As soon as you invest time and energy into creating a seascape in the Water Zone with magnetic letters and pretty sprinkles float-ing in the food-coloured water you are turning your back on skill-focused learning. If you find yourself doing circle time because that's what you do every week on a Wednesday afternoon before home time, then you are turn-ing your back. If your children are operating in a factory line waiting for the TA to 'help' them make a Mother's Day card, then you are turning your back.

Everything, every detail of your day has to be committed to skills growth, to children applying their skills to situations and experiences, and opening up opportunities to develop new ones alongside them. Do you spend three weeks of Autumn term rehearsing your class Nativity? Ask yourself what skills are being truly developed. It's a blunt question and if the answer is either 'because we always do it' or 'because the parents like it', then your Nativity might be something to rethink.

To achieve skills growth effectively, you need to know your children's Next Steps

This is the key to enabling your faith in children to really show and take root in your classroom. This is perhaps the hardest thing to get right and the one that needs experimentation and perseverance. Children don't nec-essarily learn in a linear way; they are not on a straight line from point A to point B. Their minds flip and switch, weave, retread, dip and soar across a year. They may show understanding one day but then the next day find the same thing challenging. Our role is to persist and repeat, and above all to give them opportunities to engage and re-engage. You will find their next steps sometimes appear from nowhere. At other times they are very clear. Children always bring their next steps into their learning – their voice is always telling you something.

Clear assessment is important here, whether it is recorded in a table, plotted on a diagram, or mentally noted. The one thing that is crucial is that you hold to the concept that each child is an individual with individual next steps. Red Group, Blue Group, Yellow Group approaches cannot work day in day out here. Yes, it can be useful sometimes to put children together in such a way, but in truth each child's rate of development is unique to them. If you accept this and make each child's next steps the focal point of your day, then your children will make progress – it's almost impossible for them not to. In truth, you can find out a child's next steps very quickly by interacting with them and talking, engaging them in an ad hoc assessment. Essentially, you need to find out what a child can do, then think – now what? If a child can consistently segment words and blend them is their Next Step not then to read by sight? If they can recognise numerals 0–10 with ease, is their Next Step not to be shown the patterns of numerals 11–20? If they cannot count 1:1, then what is stopping them? Is it their lack of ability to touch each object to be counted, is it their inability to say the numbers in the correct sequence? It goes beyond that they simply can't count. We need to unpick the specifics and work on those so they can move forward.

In subsequent chapters we'll explore this idea further, but for now ask yourself whether you are ready to open your own mind to moving away from what is a essentially a KS1/KS2 model of grouping children. Can you see that children are individuals, with their own unique voice, mind and developmental needs? I think that this is one of the most exciting ways of seeing children. Apply a sense of freedom to the children *and* yourself. After all, do we not see ourselves as individuals in the adult world? Are we not aware of our own distinct nature, are we not frequently driven by our own minds to try to be different from others? If I am due to go to a social event and someone happens to say, 'Oh, I can't wait for you to meet so-and-so. You'll get on really well, they're just like you', then a petulant part of me will go out of my way to deliberately not get on with them because I see myself as individual. I don't want to be like the next person – I want to be me. I think this analogy works with children, too. They exist deeply in their 'me-ness' and it is this that we need to recognise in the classroom – we need to meet them on the level of their individuality.

CHAPTER 2

MAKING THEIR UNIVERSE THE RIGHT UNIVERSE

'I feel like I'm just treading water. Is it the same for you?' – Antichrist, *The 1975*

I love the colour grey in my home. I love grey paint on walls, grey sofas, grey radiators, grey armchairs. I watch films and find myself looking beyond the characters and the action to see what colour the walls are. Most of the film *What Lies Beneath* went by me because I was so intent on deciding whether Michelle Pfeiffer's walls were battleship or gun-metal grey. I choose to paint walls in my house grey because I find it relaxing and calming. It goes with pops of colour courtesy of wallpaper and cushions. Grey makes my home *home*.

Now consider your classroom space

Is the space calming? Is it a home for the children? Is it representing your own idea of what you think a classroom should look like, is it decorated with online-acquired displays, posters and huge intricate boards in garish primary hues? We need to begin to ask ourselves: what is it that children need around them to truly learn, feel safe and feel like the classroom is somewhere that they can call their own.

Your objective should be to create a universe that they can operate within that is their universe not the adults' nor the adults' idea of what that universe should look like. Go on Pinterest right now and search for classroom ideas. You'll find picture after picture of primary coloured borders, and charts and displays – neat and tidy, ordered and the outcome of a weekend's laminating, cutting and sticking up. All lovely, though your crafted displays aren't necessarily proven to be effective for children.

Ask yourself why you put up displays in your classroom. Who are they for? In truth, they are likely to be more for the adults in the guise of SLT, parents and visitors. They are for the domain of the Learning Walk. Your children may have the temporary glow of seeing something they've written or drawn presented in a neatly trimmed border, but that feeling will fade very quickly as it becomes another part of the wallpaper around them. And then you'll have to go again and spend time on another display. Life is literally too short. Your children don't need these displays. What they need is a universe that is theirs.

Primary colours, writing everywhere and brightly backed display boards create a maelstrom of sensory overload. The number of children with needs on the autism spectrum seems to be increasing and these children in particular are spending their school days in confusing environments that scream at them in a riot of information and bright colour. Our Early Years classroom spaces need a rethink. A really useful exercise is to ask your children to tell you their favourite things about the learning space. Whenever I have done this simple exercise, not once has a child mentioned any type of display. We slavishly put these things up because we *think* we need to. It's like an unspoken rule passed down from generation to generation that somehow classrooms have to look a certain way. Well, they don't – in fact, the adage *less is more* is the way forward.

'You think I'm still the same/In every single way/But I changed ...' Gone, Day Wave

The second useful exercise is to take a look at your classroom space yourself. Is what I have put up useful? Is it engaging? Is it at child eye-level? There really is nothing better than applying a sense of gay abandon and literally ripping your classroom apart ready to rebuild it. Take everything down – the backing paper, the printed number lines, the Words of the Week display, the reward charts, the Welcome board. Declutter. It's one of the hardest things to do, but one of the most refreshing things at the same time. Question everything that you have on the walls and in some cases that you have on the ceiling. We quickly get trapped in the mindsets of the adult world in our classrooms. We become like the playground planning team who instantly think that all children love primary colours because they are jolly and childlike or every child loves a swing and slide.

At my school we take the children every week to our on-site woods. The level of play and engagement from the children is extraordinary and there's not a single colour outside of brown or green in sight. We need to take the natural colours and bring them in. Burn the purple, garish backing paper and leave the backing boards plain brown – an added bonus is that instantly you've saved you or your TA 30 minutes' work putting up backing paper, time that is better spent focusing on your children's Next Steps.

Neutral tones enable children

There's no sensory overload; neutral tones are calming, they are Danish and Danish is a very good thing indeed. If you want to back your boards, consider hessian or sacking. These have texture and cover the staple holes, but at the same time retain the warmth and calmness of a woodland walk in early autumn. Yes, it's quite a 1970s idea, but somehow we have to look beyond our preconceptions of what adults think children need and consider what is best for them. If you are desperate for colour in the classroom, perhaps add a pop or two by revisiting your wardrobe and wearing yellow trousers or a bright green top – the neutral tones around you will set them off beautifully.

And for the record, if you're interested, my favourite shade on a wall is Lace Grey – don't ask why, it just is.

'Open up my heart and watch her name appear ...' – The Word Girl, Scritti Politti

Displays and the associated 'learning walks' that go along with them are more often than not the result of KS1/2 ideas of learning that seep their way into Early Years classrooms and spaces. Like data-driven outcomes, it's an example of top–down approaches within our schools that unfortunately remain frequently unquestioned by our colleagues further up in school.

I'm not saying that your classroom should look bare and uninviting for the children, but we need to have a sense of the purpose behind anything that we put up on the walls, and that purpose should be child-driven *only*. In my own setting, we have the approach that nothing is displayed above child eye-height, and before we put anything up we have a quick thought as to its purpose. Is this moving learning forward? Is it tied to next steps? Does it celebrate new learning?

Often practitioners will say that a child's work needs to be placed within a frame or neatly labelled to give children a sense of pride in their achievements. I've yet to meet a child who has complained bitterly or become upset when I have simply pinned their writing or drawing directly on to a board with no backing paper, label or commentary (which nine times out of ten they can't read). It still shows off their work to their peers, but it does so without the encumbrance of time spent neatly cutting and framing. Again, time spent not on display but on considering next steps is time better spent.

Too often displays can become wallpaper

We, and the children, no longer notice it and it blends into the background. One way round this is to invest in some blackboard paint. A wall, a tabletop, even large wooden blocks with a simple coat of such paint will give you the opportunity to change the text or pictures on display, sometimes if need be from day to day. Chalk is a great thing. By all means invest in colours and thicknesses if you must, but even straightforward white chalk will open up possibilities that a fixed, pre-printed and laminated display can never achieve.

And the best thing about such a display? It's interactive. Children can add or take away their own interpretations, they can engage and invest in the display – they become part of the fabric of your building. Chalkboard paint at various heights also has the added benefit of contributing to their gross motor development as they pivot using shoulder, elbow or wrist to interact. Chalk is also great on the carpet or floor tiles if you have a patient and understanding cleaning staff. Arrows, key words, footprints, trails, numbers can all be quickly drawn and written, and easily added to or removed.

Such displays create engagement; they can help each day become something new and exciting. Above all, such displays enable you to meet individual children's next steps by allowing you to leave messages for them that directly meet their development in reading, and you can do this on a daily basis quickly and easily. Children very quickly get in to the idea that they can leave messages for one another too – suddenly your display becomes playful and truly purposeful.

Not only does this approach to display have a positive impact on children by immersing them in an environment that is neutral and purposeful, it will also have a significant impact on your time. We never seem to have time. Free time seems to come as a blink-of-an-eye gift that no sooner arrives than it is gone again. Weekends no doubt will contain an element of preparation for the week ahead – that is the teacher's burden that mustn't be forgotten when non-teaching friends crow about our long holidays. Less time spent on immaculate displays and being a laminator slave will free up time for other, more meaningful things. One of those things could be to relax and enjoy some me-time. Maybe in among the chalkboard notes and messages for your children you could leave one for yourself that might simply act as a reminder that there is a life beyond the classroom.

Freedom – *George Michael*

We've already touched upon the idea of freedom within the Early Years space and we'll pick up on this thread later too, but it's worth pausing for a moment to consider two key components to your practice that will ensure that this freedom which children deserve doesn't end up in a free-for-all bun fight.

Children naturally test boundaries

That's a natural part of development. They push against the adult so that the adult can show them the patience, love and discipline that they need. Without clear boundaries you open yourself to carnage. Yes, children need freedom to choose and investigate, but they need to do that within the confines of a system that enables this but at the same time also reminds them that you are the master of their universe. They are on your turf.

Your first half term is the perfect time to ensure that this happens. It doesn't rely on you telling them the rules and then you giving time out left, right and centre until they 'get' it. Really, you want this to be a collaborative approach where you explain and negotiate with the children a simple charter or rule set that you all agree to follow with clear justifications for each point. You might choose to do this as a whole-class exercise or a small group one, but ultimately you want children to be active participants in setting the ground rules for the year ahead. Why should they walk inside? Is it right to dump your coat on the floor? Why should you wash your hands before eating a snack? What should they do with resources that they have got out and no longer need and why? Having these basic chats with children puts them in a position of control (with a little steering if necessary) and it also explains to them the rationale behind the universe in which they will spend the next year of their lives. Collaboration and cohesion should be at the heart of this process. It's a fantastic Communication and Language opportunity, too. You may also choose to put up a simple display since this is, after all, a purposeful element of your day-to-day routine. You may choose not to do this, but use verbal reminders based on individual children. Only put up the display because your heart tells you to.

Of course, children are children and you will inevitably find yourself engaged in discussions about boundaries across the year, but ultimately you are looking for the children to have a concept of teamwork and togetherness, of safety and of consequence if the boundaries are crossed. Again, children look to you as the adult to ensure that this happens. They want you to be approachable and loving, but at the same time you will also need to let them know that your agreed boundaries are there for all and that the consequence is equal to all.

There is a slight caveat to that, however. Some children will find boundaries incredibly hard for many, many reasons. It's a case of making 'reasonable adjustments' here: of picking battles, of making sure that you can bend slightly if you feel that the individual child will benefit from a slight tweak. Sometimes it can be appropriate to explain to the other children why you are doing this – you will need to think carefully about how to present this to them, however, as children can be prone to over-sharing at home (although most children just say 'nothing' to the question 'What did you do at school today?'). Patience is key in all of this. It's about making sure you try to think ahead and unpick triggers for behaviour too. This is where the children need you to be the adult – you are their 'thinking brain' at times, but in order to be this kind of brain, you need to think like a child too. Are my carpet times noisy and lacking in focus from the children? Does the walk to the dinner hall often involve lots of noise and running? Are resources not being used with care and a sense of responsibility? If so, then it's time to unpick what is happening. Are you in the right place in the line? Are your carpet times engaging and pacy? Have you considered what the children might be telling you through their behaviour?

When I was training to be a teacher in Cheltenham, I had the good fortune to come under the influence of the course leader, Colin Forster. He is an incredibly inspiring man who on the first day went through the whole lecture hall of around 100 students and named every single one of them. How he did it I don't know, but from that moment I was hooked. On around the fourth week of the course we gathered in the lecture hall to hear his thoughts on Behaviour Management. In walked Colin who stood at the lectern, welcomed everybody and then said, 'It's quite simple. Make everything you do with children interesting to them', and with that he walked out. And that was it. It has stayed with me ten years on because he was right.

Engagement is absolutely vital not only to behaviour but also to learning

Having said that, we know that within a school day it is not always as easy to do as to say, so let's consider the second key component to the children's universe if we are going to allow them the necessary freedom that they deserve and thrive in.

'Some day soon I will forget this junkyard/Take you with me if you're going that way/It's a changing world and I can tell you one thing/Time is wasting, shadows waiting/Love will slip away' – Julie Profumo, *Cleaners From Venus*

We all live for reward in some way. We're conditioned to it. We work for a wage. We love to receive love. This reward can sometimes be one we're not always aware of and it can also be tangible like money as well as abstract like happiness or being teenage-ingly in endorphin-driven love.

Children are no different. The most common reward that teachers think of is the trusty sticker – stars, footballs, monsters, fairies, etc. The problem here is that this favourite can soon prove divisive. Almost as soon as the sticker has hit the school jumper you can hear the other children in the near vicinity asking for stickers too, and then the clamour begins, and the questioning and the general sense of unfairness that 9/10 times ensues. And it's usually those children who don't necessarily day-in-day-out deserve a sticker that are the quickest to be rewarded for doing things that the rest of the class do without prompting.

A more preferable solution is to use the class charter as the starting point and introduce a class reward system. This way the children are working as a collaborative team to ensure that they explore and make decisions for the collective good. As soon as you catch children making the choices that you have agreed in your charter, then you award them, not as an individual but as a whole. In my own setting we use go-gos, small brightly coloured plastic aliens that are stored in a see-through pot. Next to this pot is another pot to which go-gos are transferred one by one for acts of positive behaviour. As soon as the pot is empty, the class gets some reward whether it be bubbles, sitting on a whoopee cushion, a go with a light sabre, being sprayed in the face with water – whatever thing makes them laugh and know that they have done a Good Thing. It's an incredibly powerful way to ensure that children see themselves as part of something *bigger than being an individual.*

'Children waiting for the day they feel good/Happy Birthday, Happy Birthday/Made to feel the way that every child should/Sit and listen, sit and listen/Went to school and I was very nervous No one knew me, no one knew me …'– Mad World, *Tears For Fears*

This is where your boundaries, high expectations and collective reward system combine to meet all these developmental needs while at the same time hopefully being open to some laughter and a sense of fun along the way. And children thrive on fun, on being happy and safe. You have created a perfect positive storm in preparation for the terms ahead in which children can explore and investigate within a structure that recognises them as people first and foremost. They feel rewarded for their demonstrations of operating within their agreed systems and are housed in a clear and unfussy room which enables them to think, feel and be.

Alongside all of this lies you as the model. The boundaries that you have created with the children need to be followed by you. If you have agreed with the children that 'indoor voices' need to be used because the children want a quiet indoor environment, you yourself as the adult need to follow their rule too. This means no shouting across the space to get children's attention or barking commands as the children line up. You need to model the expectations children have agreed on. If you don't, then the children will quickly see through you and begin to question why they should need to behave within the boundaries too. It's a very subtle thing that happens here and if children begin to have their respect for you eroded, it can be very difficult to win back. Get it right from day one and you give yourself the best chance to create something wonderful for your children, the memory of which will stay with them for a long time and, who knows, it may even stay with you too.

'In this elegant chaos I stand to one side ...' Julian Cope

The two words 'day one' in that last sentence are really important. All too often there's a rush to assess, monitor and find a baseline. Yes, starting points are critical if we are to understand children's Next Steps, but this needs to come from the Early Years practitioner not via pressure from further up the school or just because that's what the school do at a certain point in the school year. You need time to make relationships, create the charter, allow children to find their feet, enable them to make friends, and for them to grow into the universe that you have created for and with them. And yes, tracking progress is a useful element of ensuring that your children are being challenged and are thriving, but often this is an expectation based on the desire for data outcomes rather than the well-being of children. Get well-being right and data will follow, so give yourself time to make this happen and wherever possible resist the thumbscrew of scrutiny that dogs our KS1/2 colleagues.

PART 2

GETTING CONTINUOUS PROVISION RIGHT

Introduction

Continuous Provision and getting it right is the most integral part of your day. Get it wrong and children cannot progress but rather stagnate in an environment that offers little challenge or opportunity. Get it right and you give your children the very best start and an atmosphere in which they can thrive. Continuous Provision must be skills based, open ended, collaborative and neutral. It must engage, provoke and facilitate learning.

So how do we get it right?

First, we need to give ourselves a break – an actual break. We have to step back and remove ourselves from the cycle of coming in to school first thing and setting up the Continuous Provision. More often than not, we arrive and busy ourselves in trying to make each area of provision purposeful and attractive, which is all commendable but what we're actually doing here is putting a cap on learning. We are limiting children to our choices. We are not enabling – we are unconsciously telling children what they can experience and explore.

If I like playing in the water and want to explore its journey down ramps or through pipes but the adult has meticulously set up the zone with dinosaurs and a selection of rocks and pebbles with a plastic island in the middle all bedecked with foam numbers, can I as a child explore that zone as I wish? Is the adult not interpreting the space even before I have arrived with my childish imagination and dreams? We need to step away from the Continuous Provision and allow children the freedom to interpret. So, first things first, when you come in to school or your setting stop yourself from 'setting up'. Rather spend the time carrying out a Continuous Provision audit. Interrogate your Continuous Provision. Ask yourself the following questions:

- Does it promote the skills that I know my children need to develop?
- Does it tie in with interests that I have seen or heard my children talk about?
- Is it appealing to both boys and girls?

To do this, you need to invest your time not in planning sheets or carefully setting up tables, but rather in shelving units.

Each area of Continuous Provision is most effective when it is open ended

To achieve this, you need to display a range of resources that children can freely access (and return) so that rather than setting up, you are *setting out*.

Use whatever containers you feel are appropriate: if you are a homely person consider wicker baskets; if you are an Ikea goddess, then what better excuse for a trip than the acquisition of new plastic boxes or baskets? Neutral colours are, of course, best because you remove the danger of appealing only to one gender (although most boys deep down seem to love pink). Ultimately, you are looking for ways to effectively display a wide range of resources that the children can access and then introduce by themselves in to the provision. If you have a group of children who love dinosaurs, then consider a basket of these alongside a stack of wooden blocks, both of which are displayed on the shelving unit in the provision area. The children will select the dinosaurs and perhaps build a den or volcano from the blocks, but if these resources are in the Play-Doh, they will just as likely explore the dough with the dinosaurs, use it as cement for the blocks, or indeed interpret it in multiple ways. Suddenly, you are encouraging children to apply their imagination into their world. Your neatly set-up dino world on the Play-Doh table will only appeal to the dinosaur lovers, pretty much instantly closing it down to any child who might just want to explore the Play-Doh itself or get creative with Play-Doh cakes.

CHAPTER 3

WHAT PLAY IS AND WHAT PLAY ISN'T

'Play for today ...' – The Cure

Play is one of the most misunderstood concepts. In today's educational world it is also one of the most underrated. And yet it is the most vital component for development – the gift of play is the greatest thing we can ever possibly give a child. Unfortunately, the incessant clamour for measurability and adult world-dominated thinking overshadows the truly rich potential of play and replaces it instead with a stale and stagnant regimen of worksheets, structure and the treadmill of 'factory-setting' tick-box activities.

I make no apologies for saying this. We seem to offer our young children an educational experience that has emerged from the Upside Down. If you've never watched the Netflix series, *Stranger Things*, then go do it. The Upside Down is like a shadow world that echoes our own but is lifeless and haunted by the unknown. There are various portals to this other world through which they can entwine. In our educational version we somehow need to close the portal.

The Upside Down emanates from Key Stages 1 and 2, and from the traditionalist typeset idea of what education actually is and how it should be delivered. We have already explored how children's languages need to be heard and there is no better vehicle for this than play. Real Play should be from the child and for the child. It should be open ended, give opportunities for self-chosen challenges, offer limitless possibilities and endless interpretations. Real play enables children – it lights them up.

We can only offer this kind of play, however, if we are willing to breathe a different ether. I like to see children as people who breathe a different air from us that makes them behave, feel, think and dream in a totally different way from the adults around them. The ether that they breathe in is at a lower height than ours. As adults, we need to breathe this ether too. In order to do this, we need to literally get on our knees and not pray, but *play*.

Real play is owned by the child

It is not necessarily planned. It has a more reactive element that has wildness and spontaneity at heart. It can't be confined. It shouldn't have restraints. It is choice, it is vitality. Real Play is not created by the Red Group, Blue Group or Green Group. It isn't enabled by round robin activities or by a factory-style rotation of children with a TA taking it in turns to add coloured tissue paper to an adult-drawn design. Play is creativity, it is abandon. It is risk, collaboration, interpretation and reinterpretation. Its meaning is infinite and its importance cannot and must not be ignored. If your children are not engaged in Real Play, then they are not truly learning – they are merely copying and being shaped into mini Stepford Wives-type beings who lose their own identity and self-purpose.

Ask yourself – what should children be doing?

If I truly want to answer this question, do I not need to detach myself from the demands of a curriculum or state-driven expectations? Very few of us would deny that children need to play, so if that is the case, why is play being squeezed from our children's lives and from their school day? Why are we enforcing a way of being that is the antithesis of what they actually need? We need to ask ourselves what kind of children we want to nurture. Our society of tomorrow will be shaped by the 3-, 4- and 5-year-olds of today. What natures do we want these children to have? Do we not want creative, caring citizens who have dreams and ambitions, who have a spark within them, who are able to collaborate and make decisions for themselves? These 'soft skills' will define our culture through the years – respect, thoughtfulness, kindness, application, self-drive, creativity. Play and playfulness enable these in bucketloads. Yet we seem determined to crush this, to belittle it somehow. Our adult world has demands that we think play cannot meet. It's as though the only way for children to succeed is for them to put out their own spark and adopt our adult version of what a child should do and be.

As an Early Years teacher you must see this. You must. Surely it is impossible to work with young children and deny that play is integral to their development. And yet time and time again we put our adult footprint on this and drown out the languages of the child. Play is not some Mobilo chucked in a Tuff Spot. It is not thirty Mother's Day cards all looking identical with a yellow daffodil and a copied inscription in the inside. And play is certainly not enabled with coloured sashes to put on the twenty children lucky enough to get to the door first to go out in the garden or outside space. We need to throw off our preconceptions of what play is. Play is freedom, so let it be free.

'Child is father of the man / The Mother and the Wife / The child enjoys the longest days / And the longest life ...' – Father, Mother, Wife and Child, *The Lilac Time*

At some point in our lives play seems to stop

It's as though there's a day for all of us when imagination and wonder get put away in a suitcase and stored in a wardrobe. Responsibility, relationships, self-image, bills, the news, fear: our growth seems to rely on this day arriving. It's like going to the opticians, putting on your new glasses and discovering that there is a real world out there with focus and clear edges. As soon as we see this world, it's as though we begin to emerge out of the cocoon of childhood. I'm not sure it falls on one particular day, but the process of things from the past seeming 'childish' does appear to happen quickly for most of us. A child's eyes see the wonder and space behind and in everything – our teenage selves learn to blind ourselves to this and refocus on a different reality.

Therefore, as adults we need to keep children in their world of wonder for as long as possible, or at least not drag them out of it before they are ready. Responsibility to varying degrees comes to us all eventually, as do the attraction of boys or girls. Hormones kick in. So do spots. These changes bring about a seismic shift in our identities as we enter a phase that moves us away from our parents and their world and into a world of independence and decision-making. We are clearly talking about our teenage years here – the space of music, love, lust, self-discovery and preparation for the adult world.

Again, as an adult, you must be able to recognise this. You yourself went on this journey. You left childhood and entered your teenage years. If they were anything like mine, then it was a time of great confusion, ever-changing moods, crying over girls and locking yourself in your bedroom listening to The Smiths to find at least some solace in the angst-pop of Morrissey, Marr, Joyce and Rourke.

Ultimately, it was a time of life in which you most probably felt very out of control and hugely unsure. I yearned to be a child again, threw myself in to reading *Winnie The Pooh* and even making models with Lego but to no avail. Kicking and screaming (sometimes literally), I was dragged by my own body and societal expectations through a mental and bodily landscape that I didn't recognise or have a map for.

And yet now on the other side, I do have some kind of map, some aware-ness of what it was I went through. I'm watching my own daughter at the age of 15 now beginning this very journey. Now no teenage girl particularly wants to hear the sage wisdom of her middle-aged dad, so I try not to be Advice Man as best I can. Perhaps we're meant to go through this phase of our lives by ourselves and literally make up our own minds. I don't know. What I do know is that every adult alive today has gone through the jour-ney. Every adult has gone through the struggle, the resentment, the ups and downs, the loves and heartbreak. We've all been on the adventure and are still going on it now that we're adults whether that involves travel, holding down a 9 to 5 job or emptying the kitchen bin.

The point is that you know the journey that you went through. You know deep down that childhood doesn't last. You know just how challenging and hard the adult world can be. Yes, you can drink, stay out for as long as you want, Tinder to your heart's content, but you also know that the adult world has a paradoxical complexity and regimentation that makes it pretty messed up at times. So if you know it, then shouldn't you be considering the won-der of childhood and how your children are enabled to experience this when you are in the classroom with them? Does it not pain you that we are stifling childhood and in turn potentially inhibiting the next generation of would-be dreamers, explorers, doers and makers?

We need to ensure that children get enough childhood ahead of the teen phase

We need to give children significant opportunity to engage with one another, express themselves and grow the skills that they will need prior to teenagehood. And what is the one key component of this pre-teenage phase? Play. We cannot just give a nod to it while pressing the photocopier button to unleash the next series of worksheets. We cannot just tip Lego in a tray while sitting Red Group at a table to fill out missing words in a cloze sentence. If the child is truly the father of the man and we want to enable this person to be well rounded, loving, able to control him- or herself, collaborate with others, have ambition and, dare I say it, have dreams, then we must embrace the power of play.

Play creates the conditions for children to test the world, to make sense of it, to grow the skills needed to communicate, to negotiate and express their inner selves. And, of course, we're talking here about Real Play – Real Play that has been enabled by your effective environment and your considered skill-driven continuous provision; Real Play that is accepting of children's voices and need for freedom to make them heard; and Real Play that is not encumbered by the adult world.

If you know what awaits beyond childhood and if you understand the value of Real Play, then shouldn't you be exploring every avenue to make this happen? Is it not time to put play at the heart of all you do? Life is too short, dear reader, to do anything else.

CHAPTER 4

WHAT DO I DO ALL DAY?

The school day is dominated by its timetable. A timetable gives the adult world a sense of order, of familiarity. It ensures structure and gives the impression of purpose. It enables the children to file in and out, be booked in to the hall, and to be present at the right time and in the right place for all the monotony that the adult world can compose. Essentially, it enables the adult world.

As we've already explored, there exists a dichotomy between the world of the child which is free and is a riot of exploration, experimentalism and risk, and the world of the adult that demands rigidity, closure, scrutiny and a fist-like grip. Which world do children learn the best in? Which world enables them to grow and self-nurture? Which world provides the ingredients for well-balanced, independent learners who evolve not because of background or previous parenting, but because they've been afforded the luxury of time and space to explore and interact without pressure, without a strict timetable that unwaveringly lowers barriers and confines children to set times to think, act and do.

If we accept that freedom is inherently a positive facet of engagement in real learning and that freedom is a necessary part of effective child development, then we have to question the very nature of timetables. We have to begin the process of sweeping aside our adult world and creating the conditions for children to exist and learn within as much freedom as the adult world can afford.

Children do need some sense of structure. They need to know what is happening next whether it be a carpet session, lunch or home time. What they don't need is to have their learning confined to an hour of literacy or an hour of mathematics. When we impose this, we remove freedom. We constrain excitement, language, engagement, happiness and opportunity. We kill children with timetables. I come to school as a 4-year-old and I want to create a pig house for my imaginary pet pigs at home, but the adult world comes crashing in like the last cavalry and says no, put that down, it's maths now, you must come with me and count unifix cubes. Instantly as a child I've switched off. I'm being taken from something that I want to do, to do something that I have to do. As an adult, you have to recognise that this is true. By their very nature, timetables overlook enthusiasm, dreaming and desire. They bring about a world of 'You must' rather than a world of 'You may'.

So how do we timetable our children's day?

A little bit like the exercise of looking at our environment as we did in Chapter 2, the best thing to do is sweep away the timetable. Burn it. Start again. In a way, since you are a being in the adult world, the timetable is probably more for you than it is for the children.

Once you've swept away the timetable, begin by identifying the elements of the day you can't change: registration, potentially assemblies (if you feel whole-school messages delivered to the school in a stuffy hall is appropriate for your children), lunchtimes, carpet times and home time. Everything else outside of these is a choice. You can now decide how your children's day is going to look. Faced with this blank canvas, with the bare bones, you're likely to be in a slight panic. Your inner voice is probably crying out: 'What do I do all day?' And this makes it very clear that the timetable absolutely is not for your children's benefit, it's for yours.

There is absolutely no educational benefit that I'm aware of for young children to have to do maths at 9.15am every day because the rest of school is doing it. Children's brains don't work like an adult's. They don't come to our setting pre-wired to be mathematical at a set time, or to be phonics-focused for a set hour in the morning. Children think differently; they think outside our box. Ultimately, our timetable needs to balance the maximum amount of time for the richness of play with the necessary time it takes to deliver skills on the carpet.

Children need time to play

Children need time and space to delve into deep play, in which they are focused and absorbed in their own learning. Deep play that enriches and enables, that creates the parameters for children to exercise their bodies and their brains is vital. This level of play cannot be achieved if every 45 minutes or so they are being asked to put away what they're doing, and go and meet adult demands. Our timetable needs to maximise the time in which children can play deeply.

Brace yourself: the one way of doing this, of giving children the space and time to truly play is to scrap morning break. Sweep it away. Oh my goodness – the adult world cup of tea at 10.15am has suddenly disappeared. And this is a real example of how you need to put the adult world out of the equation.

You as an adult can adapt and change, the developmental needs of children can't

If children need extended time to create, re-create, engage and shape, then they need the valuable time to do it in. Your 15-minute break equates to an hour and 15 extra minutes every week, time that is best spent by the children in play. Now hopefully, you are lucky enough to have an element of space that is given over to outdoor play and that this is at hand throughout the day. A subsequent chapter will look at effective outdoor learning, but for now let's just explore the sense behind what I'm saying about forgoing morning break.

If your outdoor space is open across the day, if it is enriching and stimulating, if it is accessible and if it is tailored to the developmental needs of your children, why would you stop children from what they are doing just to gather them up to run around a playground while you grab a cuppa? They don't need the break – you do. The adult world does. We're asking children to disengage with their play so that the adult world can pause for breath. That 15-minute break each day when added up across a week is an hour and 15 minutes. Over an academic year, it equates to over 47 hours – two extra days per year when your children could be exploring, playing and collaborating together. Stopping children when they are in full flow is a developmentally damaging action. We are telling children that their activity, their depth of play is less important than what *we* want them to do.

Our timetables are normally punctuated by adult-need exercises such as the register. We often gather the children to sit on the carpet so that we can fill out this legal document. It probably takes us 10 minutes with all the hello songs, the news and the actually ticking through who is here, packed lunches or school dinners. That 10 minutes every day mounts up. It's time that could be spent playing.

Within your day you should be considering how to make a 'play sandwich'

For children to enter 'deep-level play' where they are highly engaged and absorbed, they need beyond 45 minutes. The traditional concept of the timetable denies them this opportunity, but now you have sacrificed your mid-morning break, you have the chance to create the perfect conditions for this to take place. Take time to consider each moment of your day and carefully scrutinise the skills that each element enables or brings about. Think about whether the skills can only be delivered in a carpet-time style or whether they are best brought about alongside children in their play. If play can achieve these skills, then let play achieve them.

If children are self-registering on entry, then this frees up a short space at the beginning of the day to have an input time. The children at this point aren't necessarily deeply engaged and might well benefit from an opportunity to gather and talk or be talked to. You may decide to forgo this input to begin with or phase it out. Remember, that a timetable needs to remain flexible to adapt to the needs of your children – perhaps a short, sharp, phonics session, or a shared story, or a discussion about what children want to achieve in the day. Ultimately, it must be skills focused. You may decide that your TA takes a smaller group to work on different skills. There is nothing to say that all children should sit and be expected to absorb the same message or teaching. Tailor your inputs to the needs of your children. This session is the top layer of bread in your play sandwich.

Now for the tasty bit – potentially up to two hours of solid play. Children engaging and reacting to the environment and resources around them. Then it's probably almost lunchtime, so this naturally gifts you with another input slot in which to deliver a skill – potentially discrete fine or gross motor skills. Then for lunchtime, perhaps the most challenging time for young children. The most important thing here is to put yourself in the child's world yet again. Yes, you are hungry and yes, you need a break, of course, but invest time in unpicking what lunchtimes should be like for your children, discuss the 'shape' of them with the children, talk to the MTAs and let them have an input – hear their 'language'. The more time you invest in lunchtimes the better. Your children (and your MTAs will thank you for it).

Having registered the children again for the afternoon (look at how you can do this during the last five minutes of lunchtime play so that it's done – it's quite easy to tick children off a list while they run around still). Having brought them inside, consider using this natural lull as another opportunity to have an input time – maybe a short maths skill. Now time for more of that lovely solid uninterrupted play which then naturally comes to an end for home time. Consider using this as a way to share the excitement of the day or children's outcomes, or use it as time to explore a quality text together.

The big chunks of play might seem long, but, given time, they will become the rhythm of the day with their own energy and flavour. Young children don't need stop/start. If they are to truly explore and thrive, they require an experience that lies outside the constraints of our traditional 'timetable' sensibilities.

Carpet times

Carpet times are also something that are dominated by traditional ideas of what this should look like. 'Good sitting, good listening, good looking' is often a catchphrase to be heard or seen in classrooms. But what does this actually mean? We've gathered our children together to hopefully wow them with something amazing or introduce a new skill or idea. What should our children now do to show us they are ready to learn? We expect them to sit with legs crossed, not call out, put hands up, talk to their partner, sit still, look at us when we're talking – all very admirable, but only in place because the adult world conceives this to be learning behaviour.

But if you took the time to research early childhood development, you would soon find out that boys are not physically ready to sit with legs crossed. The truth is that their groin muscles at an early age are under-developed to sit in this position for more than two minutes. It begins to hurt. Girls don't have such a problem because their bodies are programmed for childbirth and their leg and hip-area muscles aren't as tight. Immediately, we can see why boys are often fidgeting on the carpet. Our adult expectations are now defining boys' behaviour.

Does it matter how children sit? Or stand even?

Is there anything that should prevent children standing at the back or sitting with legs straight out, or on their knees? Similarly, do children actually need to be looking at us at the front in order to listen? Yes, they will need to look if we are showing them something visual, but do they need to have a fixed stare for the whole session? There are many children who don't seem to be listening because their attention seems to be elsewhere, but who can recite verbatim what the teacher has said. Looking doesn't necessarily link to listening, and if you're struggling for your whole class to 'pay attention', then perhaps come full circle and reconsider what it is exactly you're trying to wow them with.

So you now have your play sandwich: input times at the beginnings and endings of a session and a healthy slab of play in which children can have maximum time to explore, collaborate and rehearse skills. But what on earth do you do all day? Have you served your purpose once input time has finished? If the adult world is such a constraining place to be, what should we do? It's simple: you need to be Gandalf to your children's Bilbo Baggins.

If you're not familiar with J.R.R. Tolkein's *The Hobbit* or *The Lord of the Rings* trilogy, then I will just about forgive you, but only on the basis of the very real fact that they were generally perceived to be the reading realm of spoddy boys too scared to approach girls or even look at them without spinning. Certainly, in the early 1980s when I grew up this was the case mainly because I was one of the spoddy boys. Shut away in self-chosen exile in my bedroom, I immersed myself in the adventures of a small band of little hobbits heading off into the great unknown on a seemingly lost cause with the high likelihood of never returning home. Ironically, I later discovered that the girls were avidly reading the books, too, and were kind of waiting for the boys to come and talk to them about Rivendell, Gondor or Anduin and all the other amazingly fantastic places in Middle Earth if only we'd have got out of our curtained bedrooms and plucked up even the tiniest bit of bravery or indeed common sense.

So, back to the job in hand. Your children are like Bilbo Baggins, the main protagonist of *The Hobbit* who undertakes a long, precarious journey to reclaim the Lonely Mountain and its hoard of dwarf treasure from the dragon Smaug.

Treasure at the end

To me, this sums up your children's experiences – there is the treasure at the end of their tale, the treasure of self-development and a singing heart. Along the way there are many perils and pitfalls to overcome. In *The Hobbit*, Bilbo is at times guided by the wise old wizard Gandalf whose wisdom and strength is there when needed – this, dear reader, is yourself. You are Gandalf. You don't need a long grey beard or a strange mysterious powers, however. Instead, as in the book, you just need the presence of mind to know when and how to guide and to be there when needed. For although Gandalf is the last great wizard in Middle Earth with great and extraordinary magic, it is the simple-minded Hobbit, Bilbo, who frequently saves the day and overcomes the dangerous challenges that lie in wait for him. Bilbo needs to believe that Gandalf is there for him, while Gandalf knows that the little Hobbit, if he is to truly succeed, must realise that the magic is inside himself. Likewise, your children have their own magic in them and do not necessarily require the magic that is perceived as wiser or stronger.

Throughout *The Hobbit* and *The Lord of the Rings*, it often seems to the hobbits that Gandalf has forgotten or forsaken them. Chapters go by when we hear nothing of him before he arrives to lend a hand. I'm not suggesting for one moment that this is your role across the day, however. Disappearing for hours on end is certainly not what I'm advocating. What I am trying to show you, however, is that flipping how you perceive children, as we have discussed in previous chapters, enables you to take on a new role, one that although it doesn't involve an arduous trek through the wastelands of Mordor where every moment has danger or surprise around every corner in which you come sweeping on your mighty steed Shadowfax, does bring you an equally exciting new self-perception that will fill you with energy, light and vigour.

'I am not a teacher, I am not a teacher ...'

So, first repeat after me: 'I am not a teacher, I am not a teacher ...' Let it become your mantra. Yes, of course you are a teacher, but in reality you are way, way more than that. A teacher represents an imparting of knowledge, of filling minds, of being top-down. We can never work effectively with young children if we perceive ourselves this way and to change this we should first start with our vocabulary about ourselves. I much prefer the label 'facilitator'. A facilitator enables, they listen, they react, they take in what others say, they guide when necessary, challenge when appropriate and are often at the heart of situations that require open communication, negotiation and positive action. This simple shift in what we call ourselves can have a massive impact. It can enable us to break the traditional model of 'teaching' and open up our minds to the voices and actions of the children around us. A 'teacher' is self-reflective because their performance management or SLT demand it. A facilitator reflects more naturally and easily, knowing that the path they follow is led by their children and not by the grip of the adult world.

CHAPTER 5

SERIOUSLY, WHAT DO I DO ALL DAY?

So, as facilitator, what do you do all day? We've already seen that part of your time within the play sandwich involves an element of skills sharing within a carpet-time style session. Now to consider your role within the meaty (or Quorny) bit within the sandwich. We'll get to the nitty-gritty in the next chapter, but for now here's a brief summary, in no particular order, of what you might find yourself doing. Some of the points might feel contradictory to what I may have said about play or childhood, but bear with me, all will become clear.

Observing

There was once a series of TV adverts in the mid 1970s called the Green Cross Code aimed at keeping children safe when crossing the road. 'Stop, Look and Listen' was its key message. The adverts were made even cooler because they featured David Prowse, who went on to play the role of Darth Vader in *Star Wars*.

'Stop, Look and Listen' would be a key message in Early Years, too. Too often we feel that we need to be in and among children all the time. We seem hell-bent on baseline assessments that then lead us in to a diet of gap-filling and instruction-giving. 'This is what they don't know, so this is what I now need to teach ... ' Teaching, directing and planning then all get underway, making us speed headlong term to term while our children struggle on to develop in the face of this torrent of inputs, interventions and planned activity. Better that we take the time to stand back and watch, get to know what makes our children tick and take on board what they are teaching us. We cannot hear children's voices if we are too busy talking ourselves. Stop, look and listen.

Collaborating

We were born to be social animals. We are defined by those around us, by our early interactions first with our parents, our siblings and family, and then by our interactions with our peers. As an adult, you need to provide the conditions for children to develop the necessary skills so that they can communicate their needs effectively, negotiate, plan, create and challenge one another. All these skills unfortunately lie outside the adult world requirement for measurability in educational outcomes, but the irony is that they are the bedrock for these. The conditions can only truly come about if your provision is large scale and supports dialogue, sharing and opportunities to have interactions with more than two or three children.

Inspiring

Yes, children are full of magic and yes, they have a voice and dreams and energy that adults can only remember as a faint. echo. But children also need an inspirational environment that changes and includes quirky objects and things that lie outside the ordinary. They need to hear words that are strange and alluring, hear stories that open up new worlds of imagination and wonder; they need drama and songs, adventure and the great outdoors. These are what you can bring every single day. Think like a child to be like a child. Consider what resources can be made available that can be interpreted, that lend themselves to enquiry and wondering. We want children to use their inquisitive mind, to apply their skills and approach with their physicality. Every day should have a richness that lights up your children. You should be able to know that when they go home and their parents ask what they did at school today and they say 'nothing', they are saying it because they're unable to explain to adults all the magical things that happened and they wouldn't understand anyway.

Challenging

The concept of challenge is an odd one. It's a concept that to many seems to lie within the adult world. Read any Ofsted publication and somewhere along the way you'll stumble across the idea of adults providing challenge to children. This idea of challenge is rooted in the adult world. Not for a moment does it recognise that children are more than capable of choosing their own 'challenge', that they are forever challenging themselves. The adult world just doesn't recognise it or interpret it this way. If you walk into a setting and find Reception age children crawling on the floor you might immediately think 'Ermagerd, what are these children doing?' But you do this because you have an adult perception of what a classroom is, what children should be doing in that classroom and what crawling is. We think it's babyish, that it isn't 'learning', that it isn't 'challenging'. But what if you saw beyond the adult world and started to consider that crawling is vital to physical development because it strengthens core muscles that will eventually support their sitting and their ability to control their bodies so that they can listen and concentrate. What if the children had created a crawling game that involved role play or racing using ordinal numbers, or were talking to negotiate rules? Do adults take the time to 'stop, look and listen'? Frequently, the answer is no. Instead, we rush to judge with our preconceived ideas of challenge and learning. Once in our garden I found several children swinging planks while other children threw stones at them. In I rushed, all guns blazing, only to discover that they had invented a game of golf with an intricate scoring system and a negotiated safety rule for turn taking.

Upcycling

However, some play can border on the edge of being unsafe or tipping over into crossing set boundaries. Your role here is then to be responsible for upcycling play. Take the time to find out what children are trying to achieve in their play, and discuss what they might be able to do to still achieve the same outcome but safely or within the setting's boundaries. In the above example I decided to replace the stones the children were throwing with soft balls. We talked about staying safe and why throwing stones might hurt someone or teach younger children to throw stones. Could they think of something else to throw that would enable the game to continue? Where could they find these things? How might it change the game? Deciding that it would add to the game (the different coloured balls would be worth different points), the children went on to play for around 40 minutes, finally ending the game by digging a large hole and hitting the balls in point order into it, the final golden ball going in with all the joy of the final round of the Ryder Cup. Always be on the eye out for opportunities to upcycle play, but do so with the sense of trust that children generally do know what they're doing. Don't always impose challenge because it's a sure-fire way to switch a child off, and we all know that it's harder to switch that light back on once it's been put out than it is to let it brighten a room of its own accord.

Refreshing

Children make mess. It's part of play. They're focused on their goal or intended outcome and frequently the space around them becomes strewn with cardboard tubes, strips of paper, pencils, and various other flotsam and jetsam. To an adult eye, it seems that a zombie apocalypse has dawned, leaving a trail of destruction in its wake. Again, this comes down to the adult perception of what a space should look like. It's embedded in a Victorian concept of housekeeping and tidiness.

However, children live outside of this. They simply don't see it and arguably they shouldn't be made to see it either. If a child or group of children are engrossed in their chosen focus, should this then be broken so that the adult can have a tidy space? Should they lose their thread because the adult world reels at the sight of untidiness?

As an adult, I find this hard to say because my life is normally dominated by OCD tendency. What I've learnt to do is 'have a word' with myself and relax about it. I've come to accept that mess is part of children's journey. Of course, we might want to pick up on children making a deliberate mess, especially if this lies outside our agreed boundaries for our collective behaviour. We would want to intervene in any situation that saw children not showing the respect that we were hoping to foster within a cohort. Plus, children should across the day assist in helping to tidy away the things that they have used. We don't want a situation in which you have to tidy the entire room at the end of the day by yourself – and indeed, tidying is linked to respect.

What we need to avoid is an overbearing expectation for being tidy or, even worse, linking untidy environments with a lack of learning. Your role should be to quietly model how to clear a space once children have finished playing within it. If your children don't, then refresh the space yourself. Judge whether the space can be used effectively by children. If it can be, then walk on; if it can't, then take the time to reset the area so that the next children who come along can engage in learning. Think carefully where you encourage children to build, too. If they spend an hour creating a dinosaur world with small blocks, can it be left out for the rest of the day? Can it be left out overnight so that the same or different children can get involved? If children build on your carpet space, then inevitably it will need to be packed away, but if it's at the side there is then a stronger likelihood for it to be left out. Don't worry about the cleaner at the end of day. Think of the children first. Explain to the cleaner that you want it left out and make it clear why. Bring them on board. Allow yourself to be a judicious tidier, and for goodness sake don't fall into the trap of corralling your children around at tidy-up time, shouting and clanging a tambourine. You won't like yourself and neither will your children.

Playing

Keep the best until almost last: play. This is your way forward. Play will be what drives your day. It will be what lifts the children, engages them and brings you into their world. When you play, you facilitate. Excitingly, there is a way to play that will change your life forever and in the next chapter we will discover this together. Once you know how, you will never want to turn back. It will make you an advocate of play and create within you another voice that can make a difference in an educational world that clamours for formality, adherence and all the narrowness that is toppling our children further and further over the edge of mental ill-health and disconnection.

Intervening

More will become clear, but there is also not-play. Not-play encompasses everything that can only be done through intervention. It's a useful exercise to think 'What can I achieve through play, what can I only achieve through intervention?' Not-play involves bringing children to you to have a direct experience that you believe will move their understanding forward because play has not or cannot. If a child has a speech difficulty, you will of course explore various avenues to move their speech skills forward and these, I hope, would include a high degree of modelled language through play. However, for speech work to be truly effective, the child in question will almost certainly need time when they can focus on your mouth movement and enunciation in relative quiet. This will require not-play. You might do the intervention in a playful way, but playful way does not make play. You need to continually be making the call whether to utilise play or not-play across the day. Be very careful, however, to ensure that play is greater than not-play. For example, it's easy to fall into the trap that EAL children need to come and do language skill work with adults, sharing language and books and having a stack of pre-teaching. However, it's my experience that EAL children will learn quicker and more deeply if they do so through play, collaborating with peers and being immersed in a rich environment of communication and social interaction. Such a world is far more enriching and engaging than the quiet of a small room away from others to look at Talking Book with an adult who asks questions and Not-Plays at being interested or interesting. There's nothing wrong with the latter, but there is if this is seen as the only effective way to teach language. Children are far better teachers than you and I will ever be. Again, it comes back to our initial discussions about having faith in children. Have it and they will repay you in ways that you can only dream of achieving.

The key in all of the above is that you are always considering each child as being on an individual journey, on an individual adventure. In *The Hobbit* there is only one main protagonist, Bilbo. Treat each child like Bilbo and you will be 99.9 per cent of the way to defeating Smaug and reclaiming the dwarf's treasure.

PART 3

THE 3MS

Introduction

Hopefully, having got this far in the book, you're nodding in agreement with the idea that children have a 'language' and that to get the best from children we need to consider play as the most effective vehicle through which to engage them in meaningful experiences. I'm guessing if you don't agree, then you'll have put the book down long ago and headed back to the photocopier to await your worksheets or trudged off to plan the next unit of work. If that is the case, then good luck to you and, more importantly, good luck to your children. If you've stuck with me so far, then you're now at the point in the book where I hope to change your life.

CHAPTER 6

WHAT ARE THE 3Ms?

Well, they're based on the approach that children don't and can't learn effectively in a linear way. Our adult world in education is focused on ideas of progress and being able to measure this. The pressure to do so then makes us try to shape children into a confined timetable of knowledge, a series of hoops through which to jump.

The 3Ms tips this idea on its head. It suggests that children don't learn in a defined structure but rather in a broader almost 'as and when' fashion. Children with you have a whole year to develop not just a narrow week in which to tell you all they know about shape names, for example. Direct teaching times will follow a predetermined path on the whole, but the rest of the time will enable children to engage, explore and interpret through their own senses. It maximises the play sandwich and here's how.

As an adult, you operate in the adult world. As a teacher or Early Years worker, you operate in the adult world. You can't just play. You have data to input and track, boxes to tick, measures to take, checklists, meetings, learning walks, work scrutinies – the list goes on and on, even into the doublespeak of rapid progress, closing the gap, and age-related outcomes. The adult world needs this kind of process to function and you're a part of that no matter what you think children should do or should not do. The beauty of the 3Ms is that it allows you to meet the demands of the adult world while at the same time giving you deep and enriching moments that enable children to display the kinds of learning that you as an adult need in your world.

The 3Ms are simply these:

1. Making conversation
2. Mark making
3. Mathematics

They are the three principles that any adult working with children need to have in their heads when interacting with children.

There is a bit of a dichotomy at work here. The 3Ms accepts the freedom and delight of play, but at the same time seeks to harness it for the purposes of the adult world. If you just allow children to play, then arguably you will struggle to evidence to the adult world how children have moved forward. The children, of course, will have a great time but you won't necessarily have one when your SLT starts knocking on the door. You need to use the power of play to achieve the outcomes expected of children. You know that it is the most effective way and the 3Ms will be your guide to achieving adult world expectations.

It's a little like being a play Ninja, exploiting opportunities subtly and stealthily. Your children see play, you see learning, your SLT sees data. Each cog sees what it needs to see, but it is being achieved through the most powerful medium: play. There doesn't need to be a worksheet or a learning journey in sight.

The 3Ms liberate you

You can't 3Ms with the Red Group stuck slavishly 'doing' work at a table. You can't 3Ms with a planning sheet for the week that states 'children will learn x'. You need to be in and among children, playing and collaborating with them, using the conditions of play to your adult world advantage. By going in to play with the 3Ms in your head, you are able to react to all the magic around you. At a table you are only ever an observer of richness around you at best and are subtly sending out the damaging message to children that valuable things only happen when the teacher calls them over.

So how does it work in principle? The idea is pretty simple. *You plan for Next Steps, not activity.* You think about each child and consider what is their current position in terms of the 3Ms and note this. Then think about what their Next Step should be and note this. It is this Next Step that you'll be looking for in their play. Focusing on their next steps will enrich your own thinking about child development and the steps they need to take along their journey and it will certainly help you see the little steps that children need to acquire. Ofsted seems to love the idea of being 'forensic', but don't be forensic for their sake, be forensic for your children – unpick what is truly blocking them, what challenges they find hard, what they are not hearing or processing. Each child's next steps might look very different from the next or there might be similarities. It matters little because the 3Ms sees children as independent one-offs.

For each child there will therefore be three potential learning outcomes that I could look for or enable, but with the understanding that if a different opportunity emerges for the development for a different next step, I don't shut this down. I bear in mind that my role is to facilitate, not to close down children into my narrow way of thinking. Recording children's next steps on a table is really only there to reinforce my perception of each child – it's certainly not a 'children must, or children will' type of checklist.

The next step is then to roll up your sleeves and go and get stuck in to play

Take the 3Ms with you in your head or have them in front of you if need be. The 3Ms act as a sort of map guiding you through the play landscape. They point you in a certain direction and, like any good map, it doesn't try to change the landscape, it merely channels you through it. The play before you will be varied and full of energy, of dreams and ideas, of choices and collaborations. Some of the things you will encounter will undoubtedly be beyond anything that your adult brain could have possibly planned. But that's the beauty of the 3Ms – it isn't trying to destroy or change or negate anything that it comes across. Instead, it will enrich, feed off and nurture. It will create even deeper play from one day to the next. You're not pulling children away from play. Instead, you are being pulled in to children's play.

By going in to play with 3Ms-led next steps, this will enable you to differentiate learning in its truest sense. A group of children building a castle with large wooden bricks will have most likely a range of next steps. Having these alongside the 3Ms will enable you to go into that play and skilfully, and with real meaning move each child forward by introducing their next step within that play. The beauty of this approach is that the 'lower attaining' children see the outcomes of the 'higher attaining' children, which can act as motivation and a model while the higher achieving children get to see the needs of the lower attaining children. After a few times – wouldn't you know it – the higher attaining children are lending their expertise to the others to enable them. Children don't then work in isolation but in a collegiate way that upskills one another in differing ways.

There is a real sense within many schools of trying to create an ethos of 'Learning without limits', but the 3Ms when applied in this way produces it instantly. No child's learning is being capped by being grouped or by being given a set task. Instead, their own play with all its richness and deeper level thinking creates its own challenge, its own progress. There is a huge amount of independent learning here – it remains boundless and open-ended. The 3Ms retains this magic and reconfirms the infinite possibilities of play.

Tracking each child's next steps through the 3Ms

By tracking each child's next steps through the 3Ms, you will also of course be providing solid evidence of their progress for the microscope of the adult world. As each new next step emerges, you'll have a true sense of their development, which is what the adult world wants to see. Sometimes, you may have to go back a step with some children. If there's a block for them, try to unearth what pre-skills they need to work on. There's no harm in this. As we've already discussed, child development must not be seen as linear. It interweaves, waxes and wanes, and it's the role of the facilitator to recognise this and use play skilfully to reshape understanding or clear misconceptions. Sometimes this might require not-play, but in the first instance we should be looking to utilise play at the vanguard of our learning experiences for children.

To know next steps, you will need to have a firm grip of the expectations of both the EYFS and of child development generally. You're not considering the how but the what. If you know this inside out, then next steps will be very obvious for you as children move through the year. If you're unclear, then it will be harder for you to plot what needs to happen next. It's a good idea to think 'They can do this, but so what? What's next?' Sometimes the answer isn't necessarily documented for you to look up and know. Sometimes you might need to rely on common sense or intuition. If a child cannot get past a particular next step, then why is this? What do they need to work on next?

Working in this way is also a really effective way of producing data. The adult world expects, so we have to deliver. Using next steps in the following way can be really empowering. On a simple spreadsheet of the children's names, think about their 3Ms starting points in September. Are you confident that the skills you've seen so far will be a foundation from which they can achieve Good Level of Development? If so, then highlight their name. These are the children you are confident will have the independence and skills base to achieve. These are your touchpaper children. You just need to strike the match of phonics, for example, and they will revel in acquiring and applying new skills. The ones who you haven't highlighted now need a mini commentary of why you haven't highlighted them. This will now get you thinking about their next steps and how you might need to interact with them over the year.

Make these names known to your SLT as soon as you have them. Get them on the school's radar. Some may be SEN, some may have speech difficulties or behavioural challenges, but make sure that you are not alone in unpicking their needs. You are not tracking progress here, but becoming conscious of the blockers to progress. Many teachers I know are great at tracking progress with off-the-shelf EYFS data programs, but they miss the real early-on-in-the-term understanding of blocks to the very progress they are attempting to track. Flipping it on its head by making projections and then working backwards is far more effective in determining what children need and this, of course, ties in neatly with next steps and the 3Ms, and I can guarantee that your SLT members will appreciate your foresight.

So how does this change your life?

It does it in many ways. First, you will have the deep and self-enriching knowledge that you are giving your children the very best Early Years experience by allowing them the one thing that increasingly they are being denied: play. You are feeding them with a diet of connectivity and growth that cannot be achieved in any other way. There is a real delight in this. You will be teaching children with a sense of integrity and with true passion. If you believe in play, then the vehicle of 3Ms enables this.

You will find yourself coming into your setting with a real anticipation and an eagerness to discover what the day will unfold for you. The children will bring their magic into your life, and surely there is no greater magic? Your day has a glorious potential, an open-endedness that matches the children's. Each day will bring its own sense of creativity, drama, discovery and delight.

What could be better for your soul and for your own sense of purpose? No one wants a machine-like existence; each day should bring about its own new adventure. If for one moment you dare to dream in this way, then perhaps consider Loris Malaguzzi's *The One Hundred Languages of Children* and apply it to your adult self. Do you not have a language, a song to sing, a passion for children and their growth? Then join with the children in their song and together enter into each new day with a joyfulness that can only be brought into being by play and playfulness.

This will be another change to your life. The children will form tighter and more meaningful bonds with you when you 3Ms. You aren't above them, you are being like them. Yes, they know that you are in control and are keeping them safe and these feelings are very important to children, but they also need to know that you have empathy and love for them. I think children are very quick to see through adults if their words or actions are disingenuous. By getting down into the children's ether, you are joining them through a special bond that is not founded on 'pleasing the teacher' or on fear, but on a deep link through shared experience.

The other area in which your life will change will be your own work/life balance. As we've already seen, the main key to efficient Early Years practice is continuous provision that enables, provokes, challenges and nurtures. Perfecting this through resource-hunting can be time-consuming as is the initial reassessment of your setting layout, the timetable and, of course, any 3Ms training that you will need to do with your staff team. However, once these are in place, then you should find that your life takes on a new course.

The 3Ms does not rely on weekly planning

The 3Ms does not rely on weekly planning other than your next steps and your carpet times. Since you are enabling children to interpret their environment, then the majority of your day is unplanned. It has to be, otherwise your children are not playing. Yes, there will be not-play elements to plan too, but you should find that your weekends and evenings slowly become your own. This is not being unprofessional or lazy or uncaring. This is about having time to refresh yourself, grow your own sense of being. All too often as EY teachers, we fall into a trap of feeling obligated to work in our evenings, but this doesn't have to be the case.

At the very least you will have a sense of being in control of your time outside school. Not only will your body and brain thank you, but so will your family, your team and ultimately the children in your setting. You will regain a sense of vigour and energy, you'll sleep better, work better and even, dare I say it, live better.

So play is not only good for children, it's good for those of us in the adult world too.

We'll go on to explore 3Ms in greater depth in subsequent chapters, but before that I have a secret to share with you.

There are actually 6Ms not 3

Just when you thought life couldn't get any better, along come three more 3Ms.

These three are the 'secret' 3Ms because they are the three that the adult world are least interested in. They are also less tangible and ones that aren't measured by the adult world and yet arguably they are the three most important. I like to think of them as a hidden curriculum that underpins each and every day. And all three of them are vital to child development.

Thankfully, all three are also relatively easy to implement once you have opened your mind to them. I'll explore them more fully in the following chapters, but in a nutshell the three 'secret' 3Ms are: Muscle and Movement, Mindfulness and Magic. These underpin your Early Years day from start to finish. Physical activity, free movement, muscle development are all integral to writing success – pen grip, finger control, core strength, bodily control, concentration – key components for effective writing, but ones that cannot just be created through slavish handwriting worksheets with any degree of joy or motivation. Being mindful both of yourself but more importantly of your children's nowness and direct connection with immediate experience enables you to play with freedom, address next steps with flexibility and, above all, gives you the tools to make judgements of the play around you. The impact of Magic should be obvious. Giving your setting, yourself, the children, your play and your not-play, a hefty sprinkling of Magic goes a long way in creating the conditions for children to meet their environment and their learning with high motivation, excitement and a joyful heart.

Maybe they aren't so secret after all, but there are many teachers and leaders who seem to act as if they are.

CHAPTER 7

3M NUMBER 1 – MAKING CONVERSATION

'Sometimes the way we talk isn't all that good/We can't change though we know we should/If I could, I'd change I swear ... ' – The Way We Talk, *A-ha*

Conversation and talk is at the very heart of Early Years

It's a thread that runs across the curriculum and seeks to ensure that children can communicate their needs and can explain their experiences. It's also an absolutely critical component for acquiring literacy skills. The 3M of Making conversation isn't just about the children's communication. However, it involves you too, especially your role as facilitator.

First, it's vital that you are aware of the way you talk to children

Your tone, your body language, your vocabulary, your awareness of their speech needs and their next steps in this. It's about getting down to their level when you have a conversation, using a quiet tone of voice when giving instructions and above all trying not to shout.

'Indoor voices' is a popular phrase in Early Years and yet the adults are often the ones who seem to forget what this might sound like. Yelling children's names across a room is like calling a Jack Russell who has caught a scent. You can shout as much as you like, but they are not listening to you. Their attention is elsewhere. You need to get eye contact first, move into their line of vision and then speak, using their name first so that they know that you are talking to them. If you say 'Please can you clear away the paints, Alfie' then Alfie's attention will only be got when he hears his name.

Learn to phrase your requests in a friendly tone and, if need be, use a touch on the arm or shoulder to gain a child's attention too. All the while you are doing these things you are modelling to the children ways of communicating. If you shout, then it is highly likely that they will too.

Child chat is critical within child development, but unfortunately the adult world is often all too quick to narrow the opportunities to talk to the confines of circle time or the family box. Gathering children in this way can seem like a chance for children to share and learn together, but in reality the topics of conversation are pretty uninspiring and at times irrelevant for many of the children on the carpet. Someone has been getting painty hands on the toilet walls and we dutifully gather all the children together and in our most sombre tone give a despairing talk about the rules and how we are upset by what we've seen. The children who haven't been painting in this session aren't engaged by this. They haven't been responsible for the painty hands. They are sitting in the circle or on the carpet disengaged. Better that you gather only the children who have been in the painting area and give them a quick reminder about the rules – target your talk.

Group talk at the beginning of the year and possibly at the start of each half term is an effective way to explore routines and negotiate ground rules, but other than these times focus your communication efforts on 'child chat'.

Child chat

Child chat is incredibly powerful and is the result of deep play that creates collaboration. When considering your provision, give plenty of thought to how each space will prompt and encourage sustained thinking and talk opportunities. How will this space get children chatting? Does it enable collaboration? Is it enabling face-to-face conversation? Does it contain things that will spark? The only way to truly find this out is if you take a step back now and again and listen. Listen for the hubbub of talk across the room, sense if there are areas that are consistently buzzing with chit-chat. Pay attention to find if there are any groupings of children where talk is not happening, where children play alongside one another in near silence. Think how you can ignite conversation among these children, how you can begin to model chatful play and how you can get down on their level and play. That's not to say that you just keep talking, talking, talking. There is a balance between listening and speaking. Give children the time and space to talk. A great area for doing both is the snack area. However you decide to organise your snack area, whether you open it for the whole session or just a small gap of time, make sure as best you can that you make a bee-line for it. Many, many children no longer experience a family meal around a table, a time that can create rich conversations and innate listening skills. Having to wait your turn, hearing parents model questions and talk-ing about their day, laughter and sharing disappointments even have been replaced in many households with the silence of eating alone or with the one-way clamour of TV or tablet. Give your children the experience of mealtime chit-chat around the snack table. It can be light and fun, and all the time you are creating a sense of family too.

The more child chat you hear, the more you can say to yourself that you have got your provision right. The adult world is anxious about child chat because it isn't in control of it. It involves super heroes, gun play, TV pro-grammes, things that adults don't associate with 'learning'. We try to shut it down rather than seeking to use it as a tool. Often, what children talk about will be what they are most keen to write about. If they come to you to tell you about their family or their pet, or their favourite game, then you have a golden opportunity to 3Ms the moment.

Child chat will often be far richer and interesting to the child than yours. Other children explaining games or how to use a tool, for example, will get an attentive audience. When we explain, we are often too wordy for most children. We don't have the same command as other children. Children are amazing language teachers. If you give space for child chat, then your language-poor children will hear an incessant flow of words. It doesn't rely on the adult world all the time. My experience is that EAL children in par-ticular benefit from child chat, their brains picking up repeated words from others in a direct and meaningful context.

Vocabulary

One thing we do have as adults, however, that children don't necessarily have is a wide vocabulary. As an adult, your language will be more extensive than children's. You are perfectly placed to drop new and exciting words into child chat, and through repetition and context move their use of language forward. The 3Ms will make you mindful of this as you go into play. If you don't play, then your attempts at language extension are robotic and formulaic – they lack the 'realness' of involved, playful learning. If you are sitting at a table with groups of children day in and day out, you are missing out on the richness of the play around you and multiple golden opportunities to extend child chat. They will be creating a shared dialogue without you and without the rich layer of words that you can lay over the top of their play. Get in their play and begin talking, all the while balancing the need to listen too. As you start using play as a tool, all children across the day will come into contact with language. That is why it is so important to ensure that your provision enables collaboration and multiple levels of play as it creates the conditions for language to happen, both child chat and teacher talk.

Commentary play

An effective way of introducing language and one that can prove very effective with EAL children is commentary play. This is where you act like a sports commentator and talk about the play in front of you to the children, describing what you see using key language that you feel children need to hear in that moment. A group of children are playing with the train track, for example, and have spent considerable time working together to build a block landscape around it, with homes for dinosaurs and a pub for the play people (their play, remember, not yours).

Going into this play with 3Ms in mind and considering the next steps of the children before you, you would begin modelling the kinds of words appropriate for them, all the while being aware that no matter what communication level each child is working on, it is good for them all to hear it.

There may be more confident communicators in the group who might benefit from hearing synonyms for objects within the play such as 'junction', 'passenger', 'reverse' or 'accelerate', for example. Other children may benefit from hearing positional language as they move their trains around the track or add detail to the landscape; others may need to hear simple objects being named. You're not directly in the play, rather you are in this instance just being involved as commentator, emphasising vocabulary:

'Lucy, you're pushing the train through the tunnel.'
'Jack, the train is red. It has four wheels!'
'Archie, you're being really patient. You're waiting your turn to have a go with the signal box.'

Commentary play can feel a bit odd to begin with, but you'll find that children will begin to latch on quickly and the words will stick. It's far better than taking children off to do language work, although you might want to have a blend of this if you feel it is appropriate. Do remember, though, that in doing so you are removing yourself and the child from the richness of play and although there are many lovely picture books to look at to explore language extension, nothing beats being in the thick of play hearing children use words in that very play that you commentated on earlier that day or week. Play brings language alive – it gives it purpose and it gives it meaning.

Inevitably when working with children not all collaboration proves to be positive

When groups of children come together they bring with them a multitude of wants, ideas and attitudes. This can give rise to conflict, which occasionally can escalate. The adult world is nervous of this situation. Very often we step in quickly to separate children and give them time out or enforce an apology. This kind of intervention, however, doesn't necessarily give the children their own independent tools to resolve conflict. It sends the message that in order to get along they need the adult to help them. Children need to experience conflict. They need to develop the self-control to remain calm, to have the ability to keep their hands to themselves – and of course as adults we wouldn't just stand back and watch children hit each other. They are not McGregor or Mayweather!

Modelling

What we should seek to do at the beginning of the autumn term is to model the kinds of words and phrases and body language needed to take turns, wait for resources to become available, ask for help, or ask to join in play. Language enables play to become respectful and caring. Children need to learn that they cannot go barging in to play, shouldn't snatch, but should rather ask and wait. It's a difficult skill at times and, yes, it's usually the 'boys' who need reminding. A sterile environment that is controlled by the adult may keep conflict to a minimum, but at the same time it doesn't equip children to strengthen their emotional integrity. Essentially, don't be afraid of standing back for an extra 20 seconds or so if you see conflict arise. See what the children do to resolve their difficulties and if words aren't part of the resolution process, then you'll know what the particular children's next steps are.

Pronunciation

Perhaps the biggest challenge when it comes to communication and language is speech itself – the skill of pronouncing individual sounds or blends to form words and sentences. Increasingly, so it would seem, children are entering Early Years settings with speech difficulties and these will naturally impact on their literacy skills. The causes for this are varied, from physical development such as teeth growth and hearing delay to processing difficulties, all of which are the consequences of the individual child's developmental pattern. These often require the input of outside agencies or specialists to assist in enabling the child to shape their speech. They will often give you sheets of activities or exercises that you can try within your setting. Make these as playful as possible. The specialists won't necessarily be Early Years trained and are naturally more focused on the outcome. Adapt what they ask you to do. Involve other children so that the individual child doesn't feel isolated – for example, involve the whole class by playing speech games during lunchtime transitions. As best as you can, make it inclusive. Think about the child's self-esteem. Children seem to love word play and rhyme, so don't just follow the specialists' activity sheets verbatim – make it fun, make it engaging, make it play!

'Parent patter'

One cause that is 'unnatural', however, is the deficit of children actually hearing talk or, as I like to call it, 'parent patter'. The modern family is totally different from that of twenty, thirty or forty years ago. Family nowadays has a lot of pressure on it, both in terms of time and money. Family has to make sacrifices for parental working hours, for career, for the adult world. Children pay the price, unfortunately. They need to hear talk from day one. Normal talk, the flow of words, nursery rhymes, sing-songs, dinner-table conversation, thinking out loud, chit-chat – parent patter. There's no finger pointing here – it's just the reality that modern families face. Sometimes it's a matter of survival or of saving for a family holiday, of putting food on the table or of buying Christmas presents, but family, to a large degree, has taken the shape of a money-in, money-out being. The time that parents spend with their children has been squeezed. Perhaps all this is inevitable and much of it is beyond change. A parent cannot necessarily afford financially to step away from work. There's no judgement here. Most parents are well meaning in their efforts to provide for their children. What can get overlooked is the need for parents to raise their children. This is part of the adult world. It is a responsibility that you take on the moment you bring a life into the world.

The adult world in this situation absolutely needs to be a positive force

One of the ways in which we fail in this is by getting distracted – distracted by the housing crisis, by money difficulty, by relationship breakdown, by community, by career goals, by having to or choosing to put the adult world first. More about parents in a later chapter, but the reason I raise it here is that our choice to talk to our children and model language is definitely that: a choice. It's vital that children hear talk. A language deficit can have huge implications as children enter pre-school age. No matter what adults do in the adult world, they need to talk with their children. A TV or a tablet is no substitute. Yes, it keeps them quiet while the adult world of meal preparation, washing up and hanging out clothes moves forward, but it is not a replacement for the richness that parents can bring their children: simple talk; chit-chat, parent patter. Here the 3Ms requires you to get stuck into parents. Encourage them to put down their phones, explain the importance of a family meal, of dialogue, of quiet tone, of listening. Many parents don't know how to parent. Show them. Encourage them. Praise them. If parents come to school busy on their phones, suggest that the playground or drop-off point becomes a general phone-free zone. If your safeguarding policy allows, open the doors once a week at the end of a day. Invite parents in and ask your team or TA to model talking and sharing language. Be the best-version-of-yourself so that your parents can be the best-version-of-themselves. If you don't show them, then they'll never know.

Society includes many people living in circumstances that we would say makes them disadvantaged. They live with little prospect, limited ambition and reduced opportunities to find meaning or purpose. These people have children and raise them in this environment. It does not make them 'bad parents' – it just means that although they are doing the best with the resources they have available to them, this 'best' doesn't always enable them to see that their children are being disadvantaged also.

As a teacher, you should be driven not by career, or performance management targets, or Ofsted. You should be driven by wanting to make a difference, make a change within a community. You cannot change everything within a community, but you can at least try to put goodness in. Your adult teacher world needs you to tick the box for Ofsted *et al.*, but this should not be your primary aim if you are to look upon yourself as becoming the best-version-of-yourself.

Put the 3Ms of Making conversation at the very heart of your practice

See Making conversation as something that extends beyond the classroom. Open up dialogue with local pre-schools and health visitors, children's centres, social services and childminders. Explore how language and talk are being developed. Yes, it's time on your behalf, but the potential impact you might have can be significant. Get agencies talking, get parents talking, get children talking. Quite simply – get talking!

CHAPTER 8

3M NUMBER 2 – MARK MAKING

'I'm waiting on the empty docks/Watching the ships roll in/I'm longing for the agony to stop/Oh, let the happiness in.' – Let the Happiness in, *David Sylvian*

When we consider Mark making as one of the 3Ms, we're going to think of it as encompassing both writing and reading. The skills needed to do either have a crossover and it's useful to consider this 3M as one that involves the interpretation of marks – ones we make and ones we see around us.

The symbolic world surrounds us

It is key to communication, getting ourselves understood and understanding others. The way we make sense of the world around us is deeply rooted in the written word. Our education system puts great emphasis on acquiring and applying a child's mark-making skills. Unfortunately, however, it also puts it in the context of a race because of the expectations that lie ahead throughout a child's educational journey. In doing so, it becomes very easy to switch children off at an early age.

The phrase 'reluctant writers' is borne out of this rush to move children through each mark-making phase. These reluctant writers tend to be boys – and more on boys' writing in the next chapter. It will sound obvious that writers aren't created overnight. There is a subtle subset of skills that underpins 'writing' and without just one of them, children cannot write successfully.

A useful tool to refer to is the Scale (see p138). It's a series of learning blocks that can be used to assess next steps for children and ensure that children have the requisite skills.

Let's just clarify one thing first

At the age of 4–5 it is far too early for many children to be given formal phonics teaching and have the matching formal expectations. We have a system that gives our young children a very early taste of failure and low self-esteem. It sets them up to fail. Children are natural mark makers and they assign meaning to these marks at a very young age. Then bang! In comes the adult world and begins to measure and scrutinise.

We are unwilling in the UK, in spite of strong and healthy models from others countries, to allow children more time to explore and not just to be mark making. Denmark, for example, puts much greater emphasis on social skills development, prerequisite motor skills and personal growth. In Finland, 'pre-school' extends to the age of 6. They acknowledge that 'who' a child is, is a greater need than 'what' they can do.

In the UK, we are determined to steamroller over children's natural fascination in giving meaning through marks and want to enforce the 'proper' way of writing. In one fell swoop we devalue their language and impose our own.

Children need time to explore, but unfortunately the adult world here cannot afford this. It has a curriculum to deliver and children need to be readied for this. What we should be doing is giving children time, but instead we look for 'school readiness', we seek a top-down approach that, as we've already seen, belittles the language of children and superimposes that of the adult world.

In the UK, this system doesn't look like it will ever change in the near future, which means that you need to deliver the curriculum like everyone else. You can't just throw your arms up in despair. The adult world will always trump the child's world. It's how we do it that matters, though. Let play be your ally. So let's roll up our sleeves, put the 3Ms firmly in our brains and get these children writing. Deep breath, and go ...

The Scale

Hang on, though, just for a moment. First of all, let's look at the Scale. In effect, the Scale is a useful tool to help you decide what mark-making next steps you should put in place for each child. The early blocks focus on physical development and move on to handwriting, then into application – first supported, then independently. That's not to say that you wouldn't give children experiences further along the Scale if they were working on the first block, but you would be putting energy into this as their next step primarily.

Working from left to right

So it begins working from left to right – gross motor development getting children active, improving coordination, postural stability and balance, working on the body as a whole to create a strong central core. This moves on to experiences that work on arm strength – both arms, shoulders, elbows and wrists as well as finger strength. The next block looks to strengthen fingers and hand grip, and works well with the next block of introducing letter formation movements but done using gross motor movements so that children can really feel the flow.

Most of the next block might then be taught as part of phonics carpet time, when children are taught to use their pen grip to form letters and consider the movement of writing from left to right. This then dovetails in to CVC word writing, applying letter formation to simple spellings, before moving on to phrases and short sentences. This presents the opportunity to begin to model finger spaces and punctuation as the children then move on to linking their ideas and independently writing longer sentences.

It seems obvious, but I've seen many practitioners getting frustrated with their children because they aren't writing words or sentences, but are not giving real reflection on the pre-skills. Presenting experiences for children that are not appropriate for them is a sure fire way to erode confidence, willingness and a key word in all this – joy. There is a Finnish saying that goes something along the lines of 'Those things that you learn without joy you will easily forget.'

Joy should be at the very heart of a child's writing experience. The adult's role should be to nurture this joy and bring it to life. We should be guides accompanying children on their journey to writing freedom for when children write with joy, that is when they achieve – they see the true purpose of the written word.

Joy should be our guiding light, but all too often writing becomes joyless and an act of children performing for the adult world. Once children lose joy, it is incredibly difficult to bring it back. Here comes the origins of our reluctant writers. It's no good children being taught to jump through hoops. We need to foster the joy of the written word, and in Early Years we can do this in bucketloads.

First, let's look at the necessary skills set for children to be effective and successful writers. By this I mean children who can be independent and have the foundational ability to take on the challenge that our educational system demands.

- Listening and comprehension
- Physical core control
- Instant letter shape recall
- Sound blending
- Flow
- Wide vocabulary
- Speech clarity
- Pen grip
- Purpose

The list is in no particular order of importance. If one item on the list is missing, then a child will struggle to be an effective writer and they will certainly be writing without joy.

Let's take a closer look at the list. In doing so, we should begin to discover the magic of the 3Ms approach and its ability to create joyful writing.

Listening and comprehension

Teaching phonics is something that most settings will deliver through not-play. A carpet time will see teaching of a new sound or an application of sounds. If you are a child whose attention skills are limited, then chances are you will struggle with acquiring the tools to recall letter sounds or word blending. It is these children who will find themselves in intervention groups from an early age being flash-carded. But unless we address their deficit in listening and attention then we are potentially wasting our time and theirs. With these children we need to go back a step and deliver on playful listening games, turn taking and looking skills.

There's little point showing flash cards if the child hasn't got the attention to even look at them. It sounds obvious, but often practitioners think that if a child doesn't get something, then increasing the diet of it breeds success. It's referred to as 'over-learning', but in many cases children seem to over-learn that letters sounds are not for them.

Take time to deliver these listening skills, deliver them alongside little and often letter sound games, and do so with a sense of fun. As soon as you say 'Come on, you know this one, I know you do' in that impatient tone that it is easy to adopt at times, then you know the joy for them in whatever you're doing is slipping away. Two or three times per day at least will give them a 'snacking diet' and when it comes to the 'full meal' of whole-class phonics, you've pre-taught the listening skills to at least give those children a better chance.

Physical core control

This block of the Scale ties in with the need to provide children with rich physical activity that grows their muscles and physique. We've already seen that they need to engage in this as part of your provision. With each jump, block that is lifted, tyre that is rolled and bucket that is lifted, children are unknowingly developing their central core, something that is necessary for sitting.

'Sitting nicely' is one of those things that we look for in school. The adult world links it to 'learning'. We expect children to sit with legs crossed and can get impatient with those who can't or sit them on their special seat. Giving children widespread opportunities to explore their physicality enables them to have that core strength to meet our adult demand. And for those who struggle, ask yourself what you are truly looking for in your input time – nice sitting or learning? Boys find sitting with legs crossed difficult because their groin muscles can't stretch in that way without hurting them. Could they sit a different way? Could they choose how and where? Can some stand or lean? Only you will know based on the children in your class, but ultimately the question should be, am I creating a learning experiment that is inclusive for all? If not, what can I change?

Instant letter shape recall

If children are going to be successful writers, they need to give more brain space to what they are going to write than how they are going to write. Each pause they take to recall how to form a letter means less mental energy being focused on what they are writing, leading to confusion and disengagement. If you can't form letters to write, then imagine the frustration.

Letter formation can be delivered both through play and not-play. In play, we should be modelling writing, talking as we do about the formation we are using, drawing attention to any phrases that might help and making links to other letter shapes. In not-play, we should be delivering letter formation as part of our carpet times with an emphasis on 'having a go' – we need to maintain an atmosphere of playfulness and praising the effort. Try to avoid negative terms when speaking about letter formation.

Sound blending

Knowledge of letter sounds needs to be coupled with the skill of hearing individual sounds and then blending them together to form the word. This is a skill that can be rehearsed with younger children to train the ear to hear sounds in words. If a child cannot hear them or blend, it will be almost impossible for them to be a writer unless they have the ability to see words and recall their spelling as a sight word.

Like letter recognition, a diet of little and often will go a long way and, if this is delivered in a playful way, then all the better. Practising this with a mix of blenders and non-blenders at home time or in a transition gives the non-blenders experience of their peers, demonstrating the skill as well as retaining their self-esteem because they're not being pulled away across the day to practise. Making this as fun as possible is the key here, because it can be very frustrating as an adult.

Flow

Writing can be seen as being like a river. There's an undercurrent of the brain, recalling sounds, letter formation and the 'what am I writing?'. If these are quickly recalled, then writing has flow. But should there need to be a pause or a distraction, then the river can dam pretty quickly. To get the flow, children need a diet of speed letter-writing, then CVC words, then phrases, then on to sentences. It's like moving from water drops to puddles, to streams, to rivers. Our next steps planning is key here, giving children the opportunity to exercise their current skills while enabling us to assess what direction to move them in. Achieving flow can be a struggle. There's so much thinking that these little minds need to process to get there. When you model writing in play and not-play, act out this struggle, make mistakes, question yourself, show them that they are not alone, that they can get there.

Wide vocabulary

We've already seen how vocabulary and language have a significant impact on children's attainment and their ability to be successful. Without a solid grounding in story, conversation, rhymes and tales, children can find it very difficult to know what to write. They find it hard to imagine sentences or find understanding. It's why talk is such a necessary and powerful tool. If only we could give more time to this rather than insisting that developmentally children should be writers by the age of 5. For some, this is the case but not all. Space and time to talk would be hugely beneficial in KS1, but we press on regardless. If you don't know what to write, then you cannot write with joy.

Speech clarity

Without speech clarity, it is very difficult for children to write effectively. Saying individual sounds and then blending them to spell is challenging enough without the added obstacle of pronunciation. Again, careful and patient modelling needs to be used alongside playful speech games. It's always useful to play these games with the whole class too, so that the target children don't feel 'different'. Usually, they are already very aware of their speech, and what we're trying to do here is not add to this. If only we were afforded more time to work alongside them. Identify speech needs as quickly as possible and incorporate little and often speech games within the day.

Pen grip

Hopefully, it is obvious that without a comfortable pen grip children will find it very difficult to write with flow. For children with insufficient pen grip introduce a little and often programme of finger and arm development exercises, all the while being aware of playfulness and joy. I find it useful to explain to the children I'm working with the reason they're doing these exercises and devise ways of motivating them. They are usually boys and although it's lovely asking local kindly grandparents to come in and sew with them, it's not necessarily the most engaging way of skilling them.

Remember too that pen grip should be about comfort. Every child does not have to hold their pen in the same way. They will experiment and change their grip, adapt their finger position. My daughter is now almost 16 and holds her pen in the oddest way, yet she has always written beautifully and with flow. Sometimes we can be too quick to try to change children; sometimes we just need to take a step back and ask why. Don't rush in to take joy away from children.

Purpose

This is massive for children. I said earlier that the list above isn't in any particular order, but arguably this is the key component for young children and writing. Without it you create reluctance. Children should be writing for their purpose, not yours. This is where the 3Ms come into their own. As facilitator and co-player, you are going in to play and model the purpose for writing as well as introduce purpose to the children so that they are motivated to apply the skills you've taught them in your phonics sessions.

The children are deep in play. If you pull them away to the Red table to write for your purpose, you are reducing them to jumping through a hoop. They aren't interested in your purpose. They don't want to write about owl babies or complete a worksheet about what clothes to wear in winter. It's dull and it's detached from their real experience. They may be able to do it, but their writing experience has been shallow and without the richness of motivation.

Going in to play with the 3Ms, not with what children will write but with their next steps in your head, means that they can write about anything based on the context of their play. It doesn't matter what they write, what matters is that they write. For boys, this is truly liberating but before we look at boys, let's consider one final thing.

The beauty of the Scale is that it not only creates a list of skills that children need. If you look at the list below it summarises the attributes that the adult needs for the Scale to truly work. All of them are in your hands. If you display them all, then you have a greater chance of children writing with joy. They may not all achieve the same writing outcomes, but they will at least see that writing is something that is for them and that can be met with joy rather than trepidation.

- Encouragement
- Comfort
- Patience
- Empathy
- Praise
- Talk
- Modelling
- Stepping back
- Motivation

Boys' writing

'Wild boys ... never chose this way' – Wild Boys, *Duran Duran*

Boys. It's always the boys, isn't it? Cheeky, mischievous, up to no good, fidgeting, disruptive, inattentive – the list goes on. We seem to pigeon-hole boys very quickly into a type of negative behaviour box. When a boy comes along who is compliant and quiet, courteous and eager to please, we often think that we'd like a class of them. Boys' names can also lead us to think of them negatively, and I've been guilty of this too.

When I first started working in Early Years, we had a group of boys who quickly became known as the 'Cee Kay Club'. Their behaviour was often poor, they were disengaged with the provision and seemingly wanted to do anything other than be disruptive. Kyle, Connor, Kirk, Callum, Curtis – it would seem that parents were predetermining their children's attitude to school on the day they named them. I still look at my class list ahead of September to see whether these names are on the list. In the same way we can often be guilty of prejudging boys in general. The adult world loves nothing more than scrutinising boys and their attainment. Any performance management or data discussion will involve an analysis of boys and the gap between them and girls. It's like an obsession. Closing the gap. The irony is that the very world that wants to close this gap is the exact same one that opens it in the first place.

Plain and simply, we expect too much from children with the adult world's demand for 'performance' and its idea that 'do more earlier' will somehow create children who all operate equally. Again, it comes down to the concept of children working at a 'factory setting'. Can you not sense how ridiculous this is? The adult world wants boys to be the same as girls. It wants there to be an equality and if we can't achieve it, then it creates the problem of boys. Yet this 'problem' is the making of the adult world – it just doesn't want to acknowledge it.

Boys develop differently from girls. This cannot be a surprise to anyone. Speaking generally, boys think differently, move differently, have less developed attention skills, are more physically underdeveloped and are, in short, less able than girls. By 'less able' I mean, of course, in the eyes of the adult world. This world wants young children to write sentences, wants them to sit at desks, wants legs to be crossed, wants learning to happen indoors.

How sad for boys (and girls too), but this insistence immediately creates the gap that then needs closing again. Our curriculum and the traditional school environment beyond Early Years is geared towards attentive readers who are compliant and can sit for long periods of time and seemingly love doing tests. Unfortunately, school is dull. There, I've said it. It is, though. It is driven by the need for children to acquire skills that developmentally they are not ready for. It's heartbreaking what we do to children, it really is. We need to take a step back and ask ourselves, 'What is it we're trying to do here and if we have to do it, is there another way?'

Often you will come across teachers who will say that they find it hard to engage boys in writing

Take a look at your local authority training programmes and you'll be guaranteed to find workshops on tackling boys' writing. It will also feature in your school's CPD. A member of staff will inevitably be asked to take on a project exploring boys' writing and they'll dutifully carry out some action research and come back with various ways to try to close the gap. By the time they get to KS2 and even KS1, however, you are chasing your tail. What we do in Early Years holds the key to boys' writing – it is here that we make or break our boys. It's here that we can either bring them to life or switch them off. It comes back to the idea of joy and joyfulness, and through your acceptance that what you trying to achieve with boys at the age of 4 is laughingly inappropriate. I say laughingly, but unfortunately it isn't funny – it's the exact opposite.

In a nutshell, boys are not ready for our traditional adult world view of school. It goes against everything a boy is and how he learns. This is deep rooted in the fact that those who become teachers are more often than not the kinds of people who loved school when they were little. They had a positive experience and they don't know what it is like to struggle or not enjoy it. They carry the traditional model with them because that is their experience and they think this is what all children enjoy. It stands to reason that if you didn't enjoy school as a child or teenager, then you are not very likely to consider a career working in education. Yet it is these people who would be a positive change within our schools. They know what it is like to struggle and be disengaged, so they would be the ideal critiques of how schools work. Unfortunately, we don't attract them into our classrooms, so we continue on the wheel reproducing the same experiences over and over. And one of these experiences is boys' writing.

Before we continue, let's clarify what we mean by the term 'boys'. Immediately by grouping them into the phrase 'boys' writing', we destroy any notion of individuality or spirit or soulfulness. We trample over the idea that boys are not a group in the same way that by forming the Cee Kay Club, I instantly diminished Callum and Connor *et al.* into a homogeneous mass that was troublesome and something to bring down and fix.

Boys are individuals

I know that boys are individuals. I know that by grouping them I bring in the darkness of the adult world. What we're talking about is the 'typical boy' – the boy who never sits still, who is often found outside, who likes to break things, can sometimes lose his self-control and is the one who means we reach for the wine bottle by Tuesday evening (or morning, depending on how bad things get). The boy who likes to please will give us no trouble. He is the reason that you can sleep at night and pull in to the school car park with a spring in your step. My own son is one of these boys, partly due to his autistic traits – he loved wet play at primary school because it meant he could stay in and do more maths – and he was a gift for the teachers who had him in their class, ultimately completing his SATs exams in Y6 with almost perfection.

The typical boy is not like this, however. He is like a wild stallion. The adult world needs to rein him in because he needs to sit, to be quiet, to be compliant. He needs to have his nature changed so that he can succeed. Yet if you use the 3Ms in play, you can have successful boys without trying to change their spiritedness.

I want to qualify here that girls are absolutely no different from boys in respect of their individuality – it's just that the adult world creates and sees a 'gap' for boys and puts great emphasis on closing it. Girls are energy, individuals, wild horses in their own right. In fact, this is where the 3Ms act in a truly amazing way because it sees no difference between boys and girls. You don't have to interact differently and you can achieve similar outcomes regardless of gender.

Their own interests

The 3Ms is all about going in to children's play to move their learning forward through their own interest or fascination. You will absolutely switch the typical boy off writing if you are continually calling him to your table to write. Get up from your table and get into their play. Get stuck in. Take clipboards, chalks, pens and pencils with you alongside the ones already in provision. Start modelling writing – boys absolutely need to see the purpose to a task. They will be less willing to write if they see no other reason than to please the teacher. Again, it comes back to children writing for themselves rather than for you. It doesn't matter what they write about; what matters is their engagement, their development of their next step and ultimately the amount of joy you can spark within them so that along the way you are less needed to kickstart writing in their play because they are increasingly driven to write for the purposes of their play. At the very least you would be seeking to make your suggestion that they write to be met with enthusiasm and a can-do attitude.

The typical boy just needs a little extra of the following, too.

Love

We have to see boys as equally as girls. We have to show them that they are lovable, that their energy and exuberance is nothing to be ashamed of. That it's okay to engage in noisy boisterous play. That superhero role play is just as valuable as any other. That ultimately it is okay to be a boy.

Modelling

I remember a child in the Foundation Unit who watched me incredulously wash up plates and cups from the snack area before lunchtime. 'Men don't do washing up,' he declared. Boys can suffer low self-esteem; they can live in households where there is no male figure to learn from, and they can very quickly learn that boys don't cry and have to be a little 'man'. They see that 'men don't do washing up'. I've been blessed as a man to work in Early Years – we are a rare breed. Most male teachers tend to be drawn to KS2. Early Years is traditionally viewed as the female domain. How saddening and what opportunities are missed by these men. Young boys need to see men giving care, listening, being sensitive, working alongside women as equals – and, yes – doing the washing up now and again without being asked.

If you don't have ready access to men (!), then give strong consideration to approaching grandfathers or dads who would be willing to come in and play and talk with your boys. I'm not saying here that women cannot teach boys without men and vice versa, but what I am trying to show is that men have a role to play with young boys – and girls, for that matter. It's important that they see them as forces for positivity and good (I know we can be slack and irritating, and annoying and childish and infuriating, but perhaps that discovery can come later in life?).

Time

Boys develop slower than girls. It goes against the traditional common view in that we think boys are the stronger sex, but it's the reality. Boys' time will come, but it's not when they are 4 and 5. Their hands are weaker, their leg muscles less strong, their processing ability poorer and their need for physical exploration is greater. Wouldn't it be wonderful if we could give our boys more time – more time to grow, to just explore and be? What possibilities could they achieve given just one more year before the adult world comes with its expectations?

Flexibility

We need to give our boys a bit of space. We need to provide the space for them to challenge, to clash, to adventure and explore, to fail and then grow. Failure is arguably the only real way that we learn. Any invention you can think of was not created on the first try. It needed numerous prototypes, stabs in the dark, falling downs and failures before success was arrived at. Our education system, however, gives no place for failure. It is driven by the pursuit of getting things right and getting them right quickly before moving on to the next topic or academic year. How damaging for our boys' self-esteem. How quickly they learn that this thing called writing is something they cannot do: that they fail, that they struggle and that they ultimately find as something to switch off from. All because as adults we need them to do it and do it in a series of steps that bears little relation to their next steps.

Writing everywhere, everywhere, everywhere

'We're too young, too young to be ghosts ...' – Naive Dream, *The Mary Onettes*

Since the adult world is currently desperate to get children writing from the age of 4 and because you cannot change this, you need your children to write. You know in your heart that it is too early for most and that if only sense prevailed and we could delay this expectation by at least another year we might give our children a more positive experience and an increased opportunity to achieve.

You have hopefully seen that the 3Ms approach to writing gives you and your children a child-centred and play-based way to achieve the adult world writing expectations. What we should want for our children is to see writing as something that is a natural and achievable goal. How difficult it is to do this through a worksheet or a table-based activity. How quickly we seem to switch our children off and make writing a chore. I've heard many teachers say, 'You can't go and play until you've written ... ' By separating writing from play, these teachers immediately make writing a 'thing-you-have-to-do' rather than presenting it as 'a thing-you-want-to-do'.

By getting stuck in to children's play, by getting down on your knees alongside them, by being a facilitator, trusting them to lead their own learning, you will have the perfect opportunity to model purposeful writing – instructions, signs, labels, words, phrases, sentences – all building on the direct skills that you teach them in your phonics carpet times. Use playful, engaging and short, focused-guided writing sessions to embellish the 'how' of writing and rehearse the application of skills that you are looking for in play. If your children see the purpose for their writing, then they will be more likely to want to do it. Write for the classroom, invent reasons tor warning signs, instructions on how to wash hands, directions, labels for rooms – the list can be endless with some imagination and by using the moment to write.

The 3Ms are perfect for this kind of writing as well as writing in the provision – writing for Lego creations, junk modelling, mini beast hunts, water play – again, the list can go on and on. Take the children's engagement in their play and use it as the tool. Sitting at a table with four others writing the same thing about a topic or subject that they have no interest in is not going to generate anything other than 'jumping through hoops' writing. It is 'husk' writing, devoid of purpose other than the teacher's. Make writing exciting. Make it accessible, make it something that can happen at any moment, with any child. Your provision and your facilitation within it should give ample prompts for children to engage in writing. Going in the play firmly aware of the 3Ms and next steps will give you writing of which children will have a sense of pride and self-esteem.

Within your provision, make a wide range of writing frames available

Lined paper, boxes, folded sheets, mini books, big books, again use your imagination. Think what you could use for children to write on all the while bearing in mind what you know they will be drawn to. If writing resources need dressing up, then dress them up. Make sure you have well-resourced mini writing tables around your provision, not just a 'writing zone'. A sole writing zone looks lovely, but it can send out the message that this is the only place children can write in. You are trying to encourage writing as something that is done anywhere and everywhere, inside and outside. My children engage in writing on smooth tree bark out in the garden as well as making their own story books with staples and folded paper. It isn't rocket science. Just give children the opportunity and they will take it. Yes, some may need more encouragement and modelling than others, but with the 3Ms and their next steps, you at least have the opportunity to make their writing experiences positive and engaging.

There may be children who are reluctant writers even before they get to your setting. Persist with the 3Ms and writing in play, but at the same time don't be afraid to put in some additional not-play if necessary, remembering all the time to be flexible in your timings and making it as playful as possible. Try to avoid nagging and pressure. Gentle encouragement and your own modelling will prove more effective in terms of improving their attitude to what writing is. Always work on their next steps and especially those mini next steps, those blocks to progress that can often go under the radar. Really consider what it is that is preventing certain children from making progress.

'Progress' is an adult world expectation and something that it loves to measure, and it insists that progress has to be linear, year by year, term by term, even week by week. Pupil progress meetings expect children to follow a clearly defined path and close their eyes to the concept that children don't work in this way, that their progress doesn't follow a rigid path. The adult world is desperate to measure progress from starting points and because you are in the adult world, you will need to be able to show the progress of your children. Traditionally, this will come in the shape of a physical learning journey, a scrapbook of worksheets and the occasional photograph.

A different format for 'tracking' progress

There are many reasons why you should consider using a different format. The first one is a time issue. If you use a learning journal, then how much time are you or your TA going to spend printing, cutting, sticking in and writing comments next to 30 children's work? An awful lot – probably in the region of 4–5 hours per week minimum. That same amount of time you could spend either considering provision, meeting parents, exploring next steps, or, dare I say it, pouring yourself a glass of wine or having time with your family. Why not even have some me-time while you're about it?

Here's an extract from a BBC article about teacher workload (online 15 April 2017):

> According to a survey of 3,000 recently-qualified young teachers, workload pressures and the impact of teachers' mental health is driving out idealistic young recruits. The survey by the NUT suggest 45% plan to leave within the next five years.

And here comes the Department for Education's response:

> We continue to work with teachers, unions and Ofsted to tackle unnecessary workload and challenge unhelpful practices that create extra work, including through an offer of targeted support for schools.

Don't wait for the Department for Education to reduce your workload, then. It is the adult world. It is the very reason that you have to track progress, test, justify your outcomes at performance management meetings. It is, in effect, the ultimate factory master.

You need to show progress because the adult world demands that it is shown. So instead of learning journeys and all the physical sticking and gluing they entail, explore how to record their progress using electronic means. By doing so you could save yourself around 150 hours per year. There's two options here: sign up for an online record-keeping app or software that will help you track children's progress, or use a notebook app like Evernote or Notebook app. Essentially, you will use an iPad or tablet to take photos of the children's outcomes and then upload these to whichever system you choose. Personally, I prefer using Evernote or Notebook because I have an element of control over what I enter and how I interpret it. Off-the-shelf Early Years software commonly wants you to input information, tick boxes and enter data for all the areas of the EYFS. You have to ask yourself whether you feel it's important to do this for Personal, Social and Emotional Development or Communication and Language, for example, or whether you can have enough knowledge in your head across the year to make a judgement. Don't forget that the software developers are in the adult world too.

Using Evernote enables you to enter photos, make simple comments, use note fields to track the types of evidence you are collecting and then share these if you wish with parents via email or a QR code. Parents seem to like QR codes because they are a bit fancy and techy. They can also share these QR codes with family. You can, if you're feeling brave, open up access to parents so that they can add notes too on to their child's notebook. Evernote is not an Early Years app, but it's much more flexible than a specific education app. The latter will generate your data for you at the end of year, which is in a way a positive but simple spreadsheet generated from your instinct, and the next steps that you've tracked across the year will give you a more direct sense of where your children are – in a way, it helps you self-moderate your end-of-year outcomes rather than relying on software to generate it for you. This might create a little extra work, but you will be more connected to your data; you'll 'feel' it and this can equip you more readily to discuss your children with senior leaders and parents too.

The other even more important reason for not using physical learning journeys is that they are obstructive to play-based learning. A book doesn't represent playfulness. If you are deep in play in a café, for example, and see the opportunity for children to write labels, recipes or order lists, then loose paper of whatever template your children might want to use or even blank paper for that matter can be written on immediately with high engagement and with little interruption in the play. This writing will add to the environment and offer reading opportunities too for children coming into the play. It comes alive because children write for a purpose and see you giving value to their outcomes by displaying it within the play. You are not taking writing off them to stick in a book later. This adds no value to the play and is writing for the teacher. Their writing has a clear purpose for them even if you invented or initially modelled it.

If you don't encourage writing like this, then you will break the very play that you are advocating as a tool. If you have to leave the play or send a child to go and get their learning journey/writing book, then you are in effect removing the richness of the moment. By the time the physical book makes its appearance back in the play, the opportunity will most likely have moved on and be lost. The adult world values writing in books as it sees a book as an edifice of learning. Yet what we really want is writing, not 'writing in'. If it's about writing on lines and this is a child's next step, then have loose, lined paper at hand. Again, if books are being insisted on, then what about the child who is not ready to write on lines? What do they write on? Do they have a choice of paper type if they have to write in a book? No. Paper that is loose and varied, that enables you to model and quickly enable children to write within and about their play is the ultimate writing tool. You also want to give children the opportunity to choose for themselves the paper that they write on and where they will stick it within their play (or not – they may want to take it home or put it up on the wall). If you take a photo of it, then it does not matter. You have your outcome and your evidence for progress as well as something to use when you consider the children's next steps.

'They need to get used to writing in books,' some will say. Resist this if you can. This is the adult world speaking: the world of book scrutinies and pupil progress meetings. This is so far removed from making writing engaging and joyful. In your provision you will have writing tables dotted around the room, loaded with various paper templates. You can encourage children who are ready to write on lined portrait paper. Don't forget that the purpose of writing should be the child's, not the adult's. Photograph their writing, upload it and use it as a tool. In your guided writing times you can, with group 4–5 children, use writing books if your senior leaders are looking for books being used, but they are no more useful than using lined paper (when you feel children are ready). Quick-fire guided writing sessions should be more about the 'how' of writing than the 'what on' of writing. You may even give consideration to writing on lined paper during these sessions and keeping a group file of outcomes – a book is only a collection of pieces of paper bound together by staples, after all. It does not give writing more value.

Reading

'Nothing's changed/I still love you, oh I still love you/Only slightly, only slightly less/Than I used to, my love ...' – Stop Me if You Think You've Heard This One Before, *The Smiths*

Reading is included under the 3Ms of Mark making, so that we retain a sense of unification between reading and writing. The two share a cross-over of necessary skills such as blending, segmenting, letter-sound knowledge and a 'mental library' of vocabulary and story. The aim of a writer is to share something with a reader. Conversely, what we read feeds what we write. It's a cycle that feeds itself.

That doesn't necessarily mean, however, that if you are a competent reader you will be a competent writer, as the subset of other skills is quite different. Reading requires memory recall, intonation, comprehension, an ability to 'picture' what is being read. Writing requires physical control, muscle fluency, imagination and an ability to 'draw the picture' that will be read. Ultimately, we are combining both reading and writing as one of the 3Ms to make it easier for you to recall when in play, and is also a reminder of the relationship between the two.

Your role in reading

In this chapter I'm not so much interested in exploring the theory of early reading. I think it's more important to consider your role within it. Let's imagine that you are approached by the Department for Education who hand you a blank piece of paper. They want you to write down the age that you feel children would be at their optimum ability to begin reading.

What number would you write down, I wonder? Would you write down the number 4 or 5? Probably not. Yet this is the number that the DfE has on their piece of paper, in their adult world. The adult world thinks like this: what is the earliest age that we can begin trying to fill children's minds with 'stuff' so that later down the line they will know more and be able to do more?

Reading instantly becomes another object for measuring, of succeeding or failing. It can be nothing more at this age. Hopefully, on your piece of paper the lowest number you would write down is 6, and this is because you know in your heart that at 4 and 5 it is just too early for the majority of children to get a sense of success when they engage in reading. That's not to say that children who are eager and ready at a younger age shouldn't be encouraged, but what we won't be doing is grading the success of the child or the adult world that is having to force children through this hoop.

In early reading, the adult world (the teacher) is trying to placate the adult world (the government). The Y1 phonics screening test (don't get me started) was supposedly introduced as a tool to enable schools to support children, yet lo and behold, it has just evolved into yet another adult world (government) tool to judge the adult world (school), a teach-to-test life experience for 6-year-olds.

What should reading be?

Let's ask ourselves a question. What should reading be? Think for a few moments. Write down a list of words that pop into your head. I've just done so and here is what I've written:

- Joyful
- Nurturing
- Warm
- Purposeful
- Gripping
- Engaging

You will no doubt have written down a similar-sounding list. Your list won't have any negative words in it. Yet, if you were to ask children about their reading experiences and to answer honestly, I think you'd discover a different list:

- Difficult
- Boring
- It hurts
- I'm made to do it

For these children, reading is a far from a positive experience. Why? The answer is simple. We're trying to do things with children too early. We're attempting to shoehorn expectations in the belief that 'more earlier' equips children earlier. We make our curriculums more 'challenging', include more content, all the way squeezing children to 'know' more. If we waited one more year, just until they were at least 6, wouldn't we have children with more of the base skills, more language, more self-control and self-belief, more positivity about school to then go on to apply these for reading?

The UK adult world as it stands shows great reluctance to consider this. It is more likely to look to so-called 'successful' Far Eastern educational ideas that are even more factory-like than explore from our nearer European neighbours who simply wait until the age of 6 or 7 and focus on the child's world, working on their sense of self, their core values and their play.

What should education's purpose be?

Surely education should be to improve lives and shape a better society. It should not be about grading schools, pressure, mental ill-health, anxiety or low self-esteem – these outcomes add nothing to the good. We seem to have created an imperfect perfect storm, with education creating societal breakdown, creating more pressure on education, creating societal breakdown, and round and round.

Reading in schools is often a great example of this. So many children that I have worked with in a variety of schools show real heightened tension and anxiety when it comes to reading. They start rocking on their chair, biting their lips, tapping, umming and erring. We seem to inadvertently make it into a success/fail thing almost straight away. This is the outcome of treating reading as a measurable discipline too early. The adult world makes reading something that children have to do. It does it really simply too. It just introduces two words to a child's vocabulary: book bands.

Book bands

If ever there was an invention that typified the adult world obsession with measuring progress and attainment, then book bands are it – an instant way to remove purpose, joy, engagement and self-esteem in one fell swoop. The adult world comes crashing in at this point in all its ingloriousness. It says, 'You've had lots of fun learning letter sounds and how to blend. We've shared lots of super picture books with you. Now have this – here's something that is very clearly going to define you and that will switch you off reading at the same time. Look, it's a Pink book ... ' Ask any child in a Reception class what they did to today and they'll probably say 'nothing', but ask them what book band they're on and they'll tell you instantly. Children know their value by the colour of their book band.

Yes, some children relish getting a reading book, some enjoy them, children jump through the hoop and make the 'necessary progress', but it is so distant from what reading should be and, more crucially, it shapes many children's perception of both school and themselves. Reading very quickly becomes something that they feel that cannot do well. As soon as children disengage from reading, it is very difficult to alter this mindset. It's a result of the adult world insisting on reading too early for most, of parental experiences that shape children's attitudes and, even worse, the fact that most early reading books are mind-numbingly, almost unbelievably d.u.l.l.

Now, you are not the government and you are not the head of your school. Both will want outcomes. You cannot change the adult world from the microcosm of your classroom overnight, but what you can change immediately is the child's world. You can have a positive influence on their experience and you can try to change parental perceptions too.

First, accept that you are going to have to use book band books. Your school will expect this and it will be its way of measuring progress alongside the TA with their benchmarking book. There's very little chance that you will be able to work in your school without resorting to using them. What you can change is your use of them and how your children perceive them.

I'll be assuming that you'll be delivering a daily phonics lesson across the year as part of your timetable, a length of around 20 minutes or so. What phonics teaching scheme you use will probably be dictated by your school because there will be an obvious need for consistency across year groups, but if you are invited to have your say, then pipe up. Your phonics teaching will be aimed at introducing and rehearsing reading/writing skills. Reading as a habit and as a tool is only really something that comes alive through practice. Children need to experience the written word and apply the skills you've taught them, bearing in mind their next steps.

Reading does need a degree of not-play in order for it to happen

It goes without saying that you need to make these sessions engaging and stimulating, and they will need guided or shared reading. Your energies need to go into ensuring that the children's experience at these times is positive. Listening to readers read, reading round a circle, reading as a group, reading the same copy of a book before it goes home are all strategies, but they are irrelevant if the very act of reading becomes dry and disengaging.

So you're going to have to work extra hard given the fact that the majority of book band books are pretty uninteresting. As best as you can, try to bring the books to life, all the while being mindful that the children in your group need to be rehearsing their reading skills. Props and games are a brilliant way of engaging children, but your delivery of these needs to be punchy and attention grabbing.

Consider throwing into these sessions some quality picture books too, simple books that although they may not be fully decodable for the children, can at least see how you read, the strategies you use and that reading can be a fun activity. As soon as it is not seen as fun, you are facing an uphill struggle. Joy needs to be at the very heart of your reading not-play.

Real opportunities come through play

In the same way as with writing, your real opportunities come through play. We've already seen how high engagement is the perfect condition for children to learn with joy. Don't fall into the trap of thinking that taking children off for a not-play reading activity is the next way of learning. Use your not-play to build skills and rehearse, but use play to truly engage children. Give their reading a purpose. It's the reason why your children write in play – you are giving your writers an audience. If you don't encourage reading in play, then chances are you'll have to dig very deep to encourage writing in play. Use the interlinking of reading and writing to your advantage. Create the conditions for children to see reading as natural, as purposeful, as achievable.

As with writing, going into play with the 3Ms and next steps in your head will enable you to differentiate the outcomes of reading with any group of children. The more confident readers will be modelling to the less developed readers and they'll also support them in their attempts to decode. If you continually group children by ability for your reading, then they will rarely see how others read and their strategies. Children teach children. By reading in play you are ensuring that children engage with it with confidence and with an attitude that they can make mistakes. If you just use book bands as your primary reading experience, you are opening the door to losing your patience with them (guided reading groups always read against the clock), thereby inadvertently eroding their self-esteem, and the children in that group will have their reading defined by the group they are in. Through play, you have so much flexibility to introduce different types of reading challenge beyond anything that you might achieve in guided reading.

Your provision therefore needs to be spot on. It needs to present opportunities for reading and the zones in which your children will play need to be provocative and provide enough materials and wall/board space for children to both mark make and find meaning in marks. And don't wait for play to get underway for provision-based reading to kick in. Use the space to leave messages, secret sentences, key words, hidden letters, inside and outside, by the entry door, on the tarmac of the playground – get yourself writing before you open the doors in the morning. Teach your children to hunt around the setting, make it exciting, make it rewarding and bring joy. No matter what book band your children get to, do your utmost to make sure that each child leaves you in July with their head held high and confident that reading is for them, and that it is something they can do, even if in the adult world view they can't.

When it comes to reading, don't forget that you're not alone. You have an entire army of people at your fingertips. They can't necessarily teach reading with your children, but they can at the very least practise it. You see this army usually twice a day, every day. It's your parents, of course.

Practising with parents

For children to improve their reading skills, they need to practise. These parents will come with a whole range of attitudes to reading and these will in turn shape their view of school and, of course, to you. They will have a direct influence on your children's attitude to reading even before you pick up a book banded Pink book. You will have to work very hard to win some parents over, but do so you must. If you don't get parents on board, then chances are they won't be for the rest of their child's school life. You have a window of opportunity. Get every parent into school to talk about reading. Some will see straight away, others will need more persuasion, but they all need to see that they have a role to play in moving their children forward through their next steps. Whether it is working on comprehension or learning letter sounds, parents need to 'step up to the plate'.

We look at parents in a later chapter, but on the subject of home reading, it is really important that they avoid one thing: taking the joy out of it. Nagging, getting frustrated, being exasperated, devaluing reading by not doing it, finding excuses, comparing book bands, comparing siblings, the list goes on – all ways that parents unwittingly wring the pleasure from reading. Unfortunately, many children will come into your setting with not only a language deficit but also a poor diet of reading experiences. Library closures, the rise of technology, the appeal of YouTube and our general seemingly busier lifestyles have all played their part in decreasing children's contact with reading books. It's easier for a tired parent at the end of the day to leave a child with an iPad than it is to read them a story book, for example.

This situation is compounded by the fact that children also see adults engaging less in reading for pleasure. I'm guilty of this in my own home, although my children are now in secondary school. The psychology of social media and 'knowledge at our fingertips' means that our phones are never far away from our grasp. Toddlers very quickly learn how to operate a phone with swipes and pressing icons. It is a world that is far more accessible than that of books. A book takes an adult to share an experience. A phone is far more immediate.

We need to explain to parents just how vital it is that they engage in reading with their children

By using the 3Ms and provision-based reading, you pass on the joy to the children, too. If your setting is awash with secret words to find or your playground has clues to read, then aren't your parents more likely to be swept up with their children's own enthusiasm to discover more?

A reading book and reading record with a printed set of instructions does little to enable parents to support at home. You need to be in and among parents, modelling your expectations, helping them see that they have a role in moving their children forward. If you have to guilt trip them, then do so; use whatever positive tactic you can think of to get them engaged in reading practice. You have to inject, then protect the joy of reading. Just getting children to the school's prescribed book band level isn't enough, for that is like giving a child a wrapped-up empty box for their birthday, a hollow gift.

CHAPTER 9

3M NUMBER 3 — MATHEMATICS

When you get to a certain age, you start being invited to dinner parties. You might even decide that the time has come to host your own. Mark Twain once said, 'The more I learn about people, the more I like my dog.' You'll probably discover the same as your record of dinner party going increases.

Don't get me wrong. People are great, but the problem with them is that the ones who attend dinner parties all share one thing in common: they are adults. So they bring the adult world with them and thus ensues talk about work, about parenting, mortgages, gossip and holiday plans. It's the last topic of conversation that often makes me want to feign a headache, make my excuses, reach for my coat and go home to the company of my children and my pets. What bugs me the most is when people say, 'Well, we've done America, we've done Greece and we've done Egypt, so we're planning to do somewhere different this year.'

The concept of doing a country on a holiday irritates me. It's just a thing of mine along with foods touching on a plate, drivers not thanking you if you pull over to let them pass, and shop signs that are punctuated incorrectly. I know, I know, I need to get out more and let these go, but when I do get out into the world of school, I experience the same vocabulary of doing and it frustrates me even more.

'This week we're doing shape' or 'Last week we did addition and this week we're doing subtraction'. This adult world way of doing maths, of focusing on one narrow area week by week, sitting over children with worksheets and 'getting them to do maths' typifies the adult world's view of filling children with knowledge, of regurgitation, of seeing children as empty and denying their language. Plus it is very dull.

Show me a worksheet and I'll show you a bin

Out of all the areas of understanding that the adult world focuses its attention on, mathematics is probably the one that children have a more natural feel for. Most parents, either knowingly or not, use mathematics with children even if it is rote counting up steps or physically counting with money, sweets or around the house. This equips children with a sense of mathematics as part of their world. Reading and writing seem to be less 'natural', perhaps, but mathematical awareness certainly appears to be more innate. Children have an impulse, but I'm pretty sure it's not an impulse to fill out a worksheet or colour in the number of balloons a clown is holding. Yes, some children enjoy this kind of activity, but not because it's mathematical per se but more because it's calming. I'm not convinced that this kind of mathematics is joyful and it's certainly not real.

Children need joy and they need opportunities for practical application of their understanding. When considering maths with young children, try your hardest to put the code to the photocopier to the back of your brain. Your first consideration should be: can children explore this through play or not-play? You will obviously be aiming to ensure that play has the lion's share.

Mini maths

As with reading, you'll be using your daily carpet time – I call it mini maths – to introduce new vocabulary, ways of applying mathematical thinking or effective ways of using resources. You could use mini maths to show children how to use a number line to support addition or demonstrate the ways of using a ten frame for subtraction. You could use it to extend the children's vocabulary around shape, around division – in fact, anything that you might think appropriate whether your school has tied itself to a lesson scheme or not. In mini maths sessions, you are focusing on a particular skill, but what you are not doing is leaving those sessions to go on to sitting at a table calling over children group by group to go over the content again. You are going to allow the children to continue their exploratory play and use this as a tool for mathematics as a whole. You are not capping their mathematical experience.

Clearly, you will have given extensive consideration to how each area of continuous provision is engendering mathematical understanding or rehearsal of skills, but this is not narrowed to the skills you introduce in mini maths. It comes back to the idea that children don't learn in a linear fashion and that they need to explore and interpret their environment. Many times I've seen children playing Unifix cubes and constructing with them in really fascinating ways for them be told by an adult, 'No, that's not what we're doing, we're counting in twos today. Take it apart now and we'll start again.' Instantly, this belittles the mathematical inquisitiveness of the children and tells them that mathematics is being controlled by the adult. It's not collaborative or facilitating leaning. This is limiting it. In this example, using the 3Ms, the Unifix would be considered a resource to interpret and then, if it is a child's next step, you would use their Unifix models to count in twos.

Engagement in play as a tool

You would be using the engagement in play as the tool. However, you wouldn't be counting in twos with them simply because that week you were teaching how to count in twos. You are allowing the children the freedom to explore, you are creating an atmosphere of mathematicalness that is unbounded. Using the 3Ms in this way gives you incredible flexibility and enables maths, reading or writing for that matter to happen at any point across the whole day. You are not confining mathematics to a timetable. Children just do not think in this way. Mathematics through play enables it to be free from restriction and, above all, it becomes something joyful, beyond flash cards and worksheets. Of course, there will be children who will benefit from more targeted approaches, both those who struggle or the high-flyers. They will benefit from a diet of little and often 'interventions' whether it be through challenges or games. As long as these remain playful and engaging, using children's fascinations and interests, you can use them as a tool alongside their play. We want children to bring their mathematical understanding or even lack of it into their experiences since this makes maths more real, more purposeful. If you are focusing your attention on your provision and ensuring that it presents open-ended possibilities, then not only will maths happen of its own accord, it will also mean that when you go into play you will see children problem solving, applying deep thinking and, crucially, conversing in a way that Red Group sitting round a table colouring in numbers of trees or goldfish or rockets never ever will. You will be bringing mathematics alive right before your very eyes. Allow maths to be practical, hands on, immersive and unfettered.

Similar to writing or reading, using the 3Ms also enables you to naturally differentiate among children who are demonstrating various levels of understanding. Use your knowledge of their individual next steps so that with little awareness that they're doing it necessarily, each child is moving forwards alongside one another as equals.

Parents as a resource

As with reading, use your parents as a key resource. If some children don't know numerals or struggle with counting, then talk with their parents, get them in quickly to discuss what you've observed. Model to them the kinds of games or language opportunities they could use at home. Maths tends to be less stressful for parents than reading at home as it's more straight-forward and doesn't always involve sit-down time with children – it can be used across the day, in talk, in the car, wherever. Parents are usually recep-tive to this and they will want to work with you. If they don't, then you need to work harder with them.

Make sure also that you are thinking about the subset of skills that under-pins mathematics – language, memory, symbolic processing, hearing, physical coordination for counting. Use these as a checklist with parents. Play Kim's game-type activities at bedtime. Can their children recall the objects? Try rehearsing one-to-one correspondence where children just touch a row of objects one at a time without saying numbers, and with numeral recognition encourage parents to tell children what they are rather than the other way round. All too often adults want children to show off their knowledge, especially when grandma calls in for a cup tea: 'Go on, Jack, show grandma how you know all your numbers!' So rather than ask children to perform, parents should just tell children what each number is as and when they come across them. It's a slight shift in the way we talk to children, but one that will benefit them.

After all, children know that a table is called a table because the common lexicon of language labels it as such. Children adopt language through hearing others say these labels over and over again until it is embedded in their developing mind as a 'table'. So, in the same way that if children don't know that a 3 is a three, then if we tell them over time and if everything is equal, they will begin to say that it is three. So ask your parents to give up their Spanish Inquisition!

As with the other 3Ms, your next steps will be critical to get right

Assessment is crucial here. Before you go pulling children away from play to count plastic bears or elephants, think whether this type of assessment can be carried out using play. Don't always think that assessment means laboratory conditions in quiet rooms with adults and their clipboards. If you can assess within the richness of play, then do so. If you feel the need to assess something specific, then consider whether enhancing your provision is the best first step. Often the best maths opportunities present themselves in zones such as the snack area with fruit, plates, setting the table, cafés, money all being usable and open to exploiting. Also remember that just shoving some numbers in the sand tray and writing on a planning sheet 'Children will recognise numerals 0–9' will not mean that any child going to the sand will do that. They won't. And they won't because it's dull, uninviting and lacking in joy or purpose.

We've already seen just how important language and talk are in Early Years, so don't discount mathematics in this. Use opportunities wherever possible for children to hear rote counting, be vocal when you apply your own maths in the administration of the classroom so that children hear your purpose for maths, ensure that you record on a clipboard in moments that present themselves: scores for games, registers, numbered list writing, numeral writing around provision, when counting out snack pieces. If you don't model the need for maths, then your children will not necessarily develop the independent application of skills that shows they have the joy and purpose of the world of number, shape or counting.

Talking of counting, there are three important words here: counting, counting, counting. Counting is a vital mathematical skill for children to take on into their onward school journey. It doesn't directly involve understanding or interpreting the symbolic world of numerals, so is arguably more immediately accessible for children. It seems as though counting objects is quite instinctive for humans. We appear to do it unthinkingly. Our brain is comforted by seeing without saying – we see three chairs and our brains says to itself 'three'. Make counting natural – again, by modelling, counting objects out loud, making, engaging, hiding or adding extra objects, children will not only hear purposeful counting, they will also begin to make links to addition and subtraction. Teach counting games that physically involve children so they see the maths in and around them – a large postal sack to hide children in from a line is a simple way to explore the concept of fewer while playfully counting and recounting. Make maths playful, make it real.

Like writing and reading, use photographs to record children's mathematical development. Resist the idea that mathematics has to be recorded in a book, file or on a worksheet. These instantly remove joy, child-led purpose or discussion. Do children really care about how many cakes Rabia has on the worksheet? Are they drawn in by the idea of colouring in the numbers of mice in the butter dish? Does it enable children to explore, apply and talk about their mathematical understanding by circling the numerals less than 8? I'm not convinced and hopefully by now you aren't either.

CHAPTER 10

3M NUMBER 4 – MUSCLE AND MOVEMENT

We live in a society that has restricted outdoor time for our children and replaced it with a world of electronics, social media and the indoors. Some of this is due to social mistrust and fear. As parents, we are fearful of our children leaving our sight. Gone are the days of the 1970s and 1980s of outdoor play, just coming home for tea, then back out again, our parents not really having the first clue as to where we were, who we were with or what we were up to. This experience is no longer typical.

Our children today seem to be tied to technology's call and spend much of their free time in their homes looking down at screens. There is much evidence and common sense to suggest that this is having a negative impact on the current generation. As a society, we are witnessing an alarming increase in self-harm, obesity and mental ill-health among our young people. They operate in a world of our making, but one that we seem unwilling to address. All too quickly it would seem that we are presenting children with the adult world at an earlier age. At some point, we have to ask ourselves as a society whether this is something we want.

Electronics and technology certainly have a place in our world, but arguably it should not be at the cost of the one impulse that is innate within us – the urge to play and to do so physically. Our physical development impacts on our well-being, our mental health and our sense of self. It enables our brain to grow, it helps us to see risks and develop strategies to meet them, and it helps us make sense of the world around us.

Therefore, if we know this about play and if we know that society needs to bring about change for our children, why would we stand to one side and just watch it happen? As schools and EY settings, we have a responsibility to try to present experiences that are positive and enriching. However, schools appear to be increasingly limiting playtimes so that they can cram more 'learning' in to the school day. They are allowing adult world pressures to erode time spent being physical because the value of being physical can't be measured and scrutinised. So this is why you're going to do it in secret.

There are two types of physical development: gross motor and fine motor. Both are inextricably tied to the other and both are needed for children to be able to venture confidently through school life. It would seem that as soon as children leave their EY setting and go into KS1, the need for physicality is confined to PE lessons and short play breaks. Children need more than this. They need the opportunity to exercise freely. If we are determined as a society to deny children this need once they turn 5, then we need to maximise their physical experiences in Early Years.

Gross motor development

Gross motor development is vital for core strength, self-control, brain growth, self-esteem and listening and attention. Children need to put energies into their body ahead of their mind. Your provision therefore needs to offer this in abundance. Jumping, rolling, catching, running, balancing, hopping, stretching, twisting, leaping – any activity that gets muscles moving and hearts beating faster. Being physical and achieving a physical outcome gives children a real sense of pride and self-worth. Children can do none of these things if they are sitting at a table. Across each day they need space in which to freely explore with their minds and bodies. They need to take on new risks and assess for themselves the conditions around them. Think about your provision and how it can enable gross motor skill. Too often it's easy to fall into the adult world trap of not seeing physicality as 'learning', but it is an underpinning skill for so much. Embrace it and celebrate it. Gross motor play is a rich source for the 3Ms. There's little that can't be done with children when they are being physical.

With gross motor, you should be looking for development within shoulders, elbows and wrists in particular because these will have an impact on fine motor development. Around your provision ensure that you have vertical boards to encourage mark making that demands shoulder strength. Don't discourage play that involves crawling – each crawl is working on upper body strength no matter how much we might want an end to playing 'cats and dogs'. Large sheets of paper rolled out on the floor force children to lie on their stomachs to draw, meaning that they must rely on their shoulder strength to draw or write. Pulley systems in the sand pit for children to move sand, tyres to roll or lift, planks in the obstacle course, water ramps above head height, buckets in the gravel, climbing walls, community play blocks in the construction area, den making – all of these things are in your hidden curriculum. The skills they foster don't want to be measured by the adult world, but you can still make them happen. And, of course, physical play dovetails very neatly into the idea of child-centred play, and all the richness of language and cooperation that it brings along with it too.

Fine motor skills

Fine motor skills can be equally hidden. Humans are born with an involuntary reflex which is also seen in newborn primates. It's like a hand twitch which soon gives way after around two months when babies begin discovering touch. This makes way for grasping and grabbing, which in turn develops into improved grip, transferring objects between hands as well as using pincer-like grips to pick up objects. Around their first birthday, children begin to discover object manipulation, the need for varying degrees of force to move them and a whole host of understanding about the physical world around them. By the time they leave pre-school, children should be able to demonstrate a tripod grip, competent scissor skills, and even do up buttons on their clothing. They will also have a dominant hand. In an ideal world, by the time children have started school they will have a base of fine motor skills, enabling them to make more precise movements and have a more fluid manipulation of tools. This, however, is not always the case and many children still need the development of their fine motor skills. Even the children who can form letters beautifully and write at will, will benefit from fine motor activity. We need to come away from the idea that just because a child has reached a milestone, they don't still need underpinning experiences.

Hands

When you consider your continuous provision, think how it can develop muscles in children's hands. What is in each zone that when children use it will have a positive impact on their grip and hand control? All of this will feed the skills that ultimately will be necessary for handwriting, something that the adult world wants to measure: pipettes, turkey basters, clothes pegs, bottle tops, buttons, tweezers, Unifix – anything that involves grip and offers some resistance. Pinterest, Facebook and the like are full of ideas.

It doesn't matter how children interpret these objects. The main goal here is to develop hand muscle, eye coordination and dexterity, and to do so in the context of play.

CHAPTER 11

3M NUMBER 5 – MINDFULNESS

'Why must we put down when we try to get away?/Why must we all grow up when we could just play and play ...' – At a Later Date, *Joy Division*

I'm not sure what you might make of the word 'mindfulness'. For many, it has quite negative connotations. It can seem a bit 'hippy' or a buzz word whose common parlance will pass in time. For others, it is a truly deep and empowering way to develop mental well-being. As one of the hidden 3Ms, mindfulness is definitely a useful tool. What we need to do is detach it from its general meaning and reinterpret it slightly for our purposes in the classroom.

Mindfulness is usually used to refer to the process of knowing what is going on in and outside of ourselves and awakening within us the nowness of our experiences, our bodies and our senses. It is about developing an awareness of emotions and feelings, and how they shape our present.

In doing so, mindfulness aims to enable us to experience the world around us and ourselves afresh.

Mindfulness in the classroom

In the context of the classroom, mindfulness has a slightly different meaning. It still involves being conscious of the present, of the play in front of you. It is a reminder to connect with the child's world when the present suggests to do so. Mindfulness in the classroom means to step back and allow play to take place, not just to go diving in with your adult world outcome expectations straight away. Mindfulness is about making a judgement – does this play need me? Is it developing in a way that I can see the children will move forward in their learning? Is it going to present me with opportunities to join in and facilitate? Sometimes we can kill play too easily if we feel compelled to lurch straight in, clipboards and pencils ablaze. We have to take a moment to bring into our mind what is going on before our eyes. There is no negativity in standing back and observing first, and then drink in the situation, the nowness of what is before you. By rushing in you can potentially extinguish play so that children then cease and look elsewhere within the setting to play, or you can end up imposing the direction of where the play leads.

It is a really fine balancing act. The 3Ms is based on your facilitation, on your adult world outcomes. You can't just let the children play without adult world expectation being realised along the way. We might want this to happen. We might inwardly believe that children should just play. But the reality is that they can't. What you're doing here, increasingly skilfully, is using their play as the tool. You're exploiting play. If they just play, then at the end of the year your senior team might have some serious adult world questions to ask you. You are using the richness and joy of their play to bring about the outcomes you need. As time progresses, you should find that your need to involve yourself deeply in play will ease off and lead into more situations where you just suggest an outcome – if the children have the skills and the joy, then you'll find that you'll have your adult world outcomes in abundance. They will see it as part of their play. You will be giving them a light nudge rather than wading in. This type of mindfulness develops as you begin to consider your continuous provision. You'll begin to ask yourself about the kinds of play you will see when the children interact in the resources and environment. You'll question what types of facilitated learning can happen within each zone and how you might use it. This means that as the play develops before you in its nowness, you'll have the trigger points in your mind to set off the thought that you can step in at this point, that the nowness is a golden opportunity. Remember that the 3Ms is giving you the complete flexibility to just be, considering the next step not how it is achieved. It's not the context or the content. It's the fact that children will be applying their skills in the meaningful context of their play experience. Children can experience any of the 3Ms anywhere and at any time. If you've enabled the conditions, then rich play will follow.

Mindfulness is key to your next steps too

Being mindful of each child's next step, of their fascinations, of their interests, of the spaces that they enjoy playing, the times of day that they are at their best, of the children they collaborate most richly with and of their home life are all vital components of the success of the 3Ms – a lot to hold in your brain. Of course, we all work differently and you may want to develop ways of recalling this information if you feel you need to. If you accept that all those are useful to you so that you have an holistic understanding of each child, then you will develop your own way. You will need to because arguably the rest of the school will be too busy with their narrow focus to consider all these elements.

When I was a little boy I went to pre-school three times a week. It was about a mile and a half from my home and since my mum didn't drive, we would walk there and back again. I was a happy little boy for the most part and I remember loving going to school, the little stream that ran its way by the path through the village, the warmth of my mum's hand as we crossed the road and the old wooden gate that creaked as we entered the pre-school site over the little bridge. It was a wonderful time, except on Fridays. I would cry all the way there, all the time I was there, and would only stop when my mum arrived to collect me at the end of the session. My mum never fully got to grips with why this happened on Fridays, but she thinks it was because there was a particular child that I was nervous of or who may have hurt me at some point. Everything else was the same on Fridays – the walk, the stream, the bridge, the warmth, the creaky gate. Yet that particular day each week triggered something in me. And so it is with your children now. There will be things that affect them. Some things you may not fully know, but with mindfulness you can at least do your very best to unpick the potential triggers so that their connection with their nowness is as positive as it can be. Work hard to get to know them as people, as individuals.

The beauty of mindfulness is that it enables you to go into play alongside children who may be working at different stages of development. It provides you with the opportunity to use a natural differentiation with a mixed group of children. The children will be collaborating in some form of play together – they will be unaware of the differences in their development.

Your facilitation with the richness of their play maintains not only the purpose of their collaboration but also retains their self-esteem. I've often wondered what the 'low-attaining' children in Key Stage 2 must think as they sit around the Green table with a teaching assistant, the same faces, the same tasks, the same nagging/encouragement. Children learn very quickly that there is a pecking order, that they are in the 'bottom' group. How demoralising we make our educational experiences. If this is the picture in your own school, then at the very least do your utmost to delay this realisation. Don't drag them off, go and get stuck in!

You just need to be mindful of when to step in, how and with whom. It's easy to write that sentence and I appreciate that it is a skill, but it will be far more rewarding for both you and the children if you go in to play conscious of each child and their needs rather than continually dragging them away to the Red table.

Be mindful of the moment and be ready to seize the richness of the now. See, hippies aren't so off the mark after all.

CHAPTER 12

3M NUMBER 6 – MAGIC

'You've got the music in you/So turn it up ...' – The Music, Cruyff

Once upon time you had magic within you. You were full of it. Everything around you was magic too. You were steeped in it. Every day was one of wonder, of discovery, of delight. The little things sparked joy. You wanted to touch, feel, to connect with the world around you. You had a hunger, an insatiable appetite for each day that arrived. You weren't probably aware of how magic you were at the time, but you saw it all around you. Almost everything had magic in it. Your senses were a riot of colour, taste, exploration and light. Animals, trees, birds, grandparents, the sky, the clouds, the grass were all bringers of joy and a magical sense of being. This was the magic of childhood.

At some point in our lives, however, the magic started to fade – or at least our awareness of magic did. It will be a different trigger for everyone, but at some point a puddle will one day, through no fault of its own become just that. You'll step round. You won't splash in it. You won't take the time to look into its reflected world of the clouds above. It will just be what it is – a collection of water. It still has its magic, but you will no longer see it. Things will seem 'childish'. One day you stop skipping. One day your grandparents seem doddery and insignificant. One day you won't look up at the clouds with great wonder. You won't see their magic. It hasn't gone anywhere. It's still there. You just can't sense it any more. You will become disconnected from the things that once brought you joy. We have a name for this process, for this slow erosion, it's called 'growing up'.

Growing up. What a thing that is. You slowly enter the adult world and leave the child's world behind. And in doing so you lose the sense not only of the magic within the world but also the magic within your very self. Again, it doesn't go anywhere. You just lose sight of it. Your appearance, the clothes you wear, the places you go, the music you buy, the phone you have, your peer group credibility, the numbers of people you've slept with, the car you own, the house you buy, the watch on your wrist, the holidays you take and the job you have, all start to define you. They become you. They take on the shell of meaning and identity.

Yet all these things are not you. They are objects around you, but they are not you. Your definition is not them. It is rather who you are, the magic that you bring to others, the connections you make and the idea that you strive to be the best-version-of-yourself. Witness any conversation between adults and young people, and at some point you will be very likely to hear the question 'What do you want to be when you grow up?'. The child will dutifully take a moment to consider, then respond with a job title hopefully to the adult's approval. What the question should be is, 'Who would you like to be as you get older?' – what kind of person, what morality, what kindness, what love will you bring into the world? Unfortunately, the adult world doesn't define success by these. It wants these things but doesn't value them higher than the things you have – the size of your TV, the designer name on your jeans, the cars parked in the double garage.

The adult world encourages diminishing magic and replaces it with consumerism. It presents a world of objects and experiences that you can buy, but the one gift that is free and more powerful than all of these is the gift that is inside you – magic. Your creativity, your soulfulness, your kindness, your respect, your connection to the world around you is all there within you and is the root of real happiness. Before we move on, know this about yourself. Do you think you are magic? What about you would you say is magic? Whatever it is, take a moment to reflect on it. Feel good about yourself. Recognise that you are magic and it is within you. Don't let yourself be defined by the adult world. It isn't too late to rediscover that you are magic and then take a step into the child's world that truly is unashamedly *magic*.

One of the many reasons that I love the company of kids is that they don't often talk about mortgage rates or post photos on Facebook of meals they've eaten. Their world is far too magical for this kind of behaviour. Theirs is a world of wonder, excitement and exploration. And this magic shines out of them. Almost everything is a wonder to behold. So use this in the classroom. It sounds obvious, but believe me there are many dull teachers out there.

You already know about the magic of the children's hundred languages and you're also aware of the power of their play. So embellish their magic by being magic yourself. The 3Ms are ten times more powerful if you are fun to be with. Your connection with the children is integral to its success. If you're boring to be around, or a nag, or a shouter, then your children will very quickly see through you. But if you are fun to be around and bring magic with you, then they will want you around them, they'll want you in their play. Dress up, tell stories, play with language around them, invent, explore, question together. I'm not suggesting that you become a whacky kids' TV presenter, but an element of fun will at least draw you into the children's magical world. You will be able to come up with your own ways of being magic, I'm sure. Recently, I've been literally putting children in our room's large card recycling boxes when they write independently at whatever next step they may be at. With great fanfare they are lowered in, to much hilarity and joy. And, wouldn't you know, the children want to be put in the bin so they then want to write. Yes, I've had to explain to some parents that I'm not binning their children and no, I don't leave them in there and yes, they can climb out. It's a simple way of delighting children and being 'childish'. Objects in boxes, animal costumes, secret messages, making up pet names for them, dancing in silly ways, little rhymes – I'm sure you'll come up with your own. Ultimately, you're trying to create and add to the delight of childhood.

And use magic as a key element of your carpet times, too. Tell the children that at the end of a carpet time there is magic for them, reward their listening and their carpet behaviours with water sprays, flashlights, zombie hands, feathers, squeezy balls, whatever you like as long as children want it. Magic can be a great and really simple way of engendering the positive behaviours you're looking for. That's the beauty of magic – it's a driver for children. They want it and if there's usually even the slightest chance that they won't get the magic, you will find 99.99 per cent of the time that behaviours will change pretty quickly.

I like to make magic seem even more appealing by giving it a name. A spray bottle can give 'magic of the goblin's wee', a rub of lip-salve on the hand can be 'magic of the garden troll', a fake plastic dog pooh to squeeze has a magic all of its own – again, you will bring your own magic to these. You can't really go wrong if you know the magic of your children.

Magic also has a role when it comes to not-play. Make intervention work as exciting as you can. If the task you want them to do cannot be delivered playfully, then at least give it magic vocabulary. I've found labelling any intervention activity 'the something of doom' really works with children. I present it as a challenge, a game between either themselves or me with a 'horrible' outcome for the loser. Presenting intervention in this way at least creates the conditions for higher levels of engagement. Even the hardest children seem to love seeing me having to drink a cup of witch's wee (water with a spot of green food colouring).

I feel as though I should clarify that I recognise that not all children live in a magical world. I appreciate that unfortunately there are many children who have terrible home lives, witness things that they shouldn't have to and have the magic taken away from them by the very people who should be first in line to make them feel and be special. Surely, though, these children deserve and need you to be magic even more? They need to see that not all adults are incapable of love. They need a sense of safety and protection, laughter and delight even more than the next child. Think back to the analogy of *Lord of the Rings* and the journey of the hobbits. If on the way to Mordor you discover enslaved hobbits, then use all the magic at your disposal to pick them up and take them back to the beauty and comfort of the Shire.

PART

4

THE GREAT
OUTDOORS

'I can't go away with you on a rock climbing weekend/What if something's on TV and it's never shown again?/It's just as well I'm not invited I'm afraid of heights/I lied about being the outdoor type ...' – The Outdoor Type, *The Lemonheads*

One day we'll wake up to the idea that children were born to explore. We'll realise that the construct of a classroom with walls and the misnomer that learning can only happen at a table within teacher reach is simply that. It's a lie we tell ourselves again and again within the adult world. Buildings by their very nature are shelters, and by building a school we can fall into the trap of sheltering our children from the very environment that brings them to life.

CHAPTER 13

THE OUTSIDE WORLD

The outside world should be part of our classroom experience – there should be no dichotomy between the two. They should seemlessly converge and merge together to create a oneness that ebbs and flows, that works together. Whenever we consider our continuous provision, we need to consider it as what works for the whole, not for inside or outside. The outdoor world offers potential that the classroom can never hand to us. Children need to make a connection to the natural world – there's nothing hippy about this statement. The outdoors must be given the same value as indoors. And we're not talking Forest School here. We're talking unbridled risk taking, collaborative, expansive play, freely chosen explorations, ultimately a deep-rooted and primal connection to the soil, trees, the earth, the sky, to our very selves. We were born to connect to nature, but all too often our children's outdoor educational experience remains limited and neutered. Failing that, it becomes an environment that is crowd control of bikes and scooters, tidying up Duplo, or shouting at the boys as they loon around out of touch and out of interest.

Yet it doesn't need to be like this. By applying the 3Ms approach, we can create an outdoor learning space that nurtures and enables. All it needs is an open heart and open ears to listen to the language of children. Treat outdoors as equal to indoors. Or be even more adventurous and treat it as even greater than indoors.

The first step is to ditch your own fear

Your school will, almost without exception unless you are very lucky, have a less than inspiring view of outdoor spaces. Most 'proper learning' will be seen as happening exclusively indoors. Stand by the truth that children need to be physical, that they need to be active and that they need connection to nature. Children today are living in a world of nature deficit. They have the world at their fingertips through technology, but have become increasingly disconnected from their relationship with the great outdoors. Some might argue that it isn't the school's role to provide outdoor experiences, that this should rest with parents and outside of the school day. All the evidence suggests that this isn't happening, and the reasons are multiple and complex. We do, however, put emphasis on the school to provide guidance on healthy eating, sexual relationships, citizenship and internet safety. A school's ability to meet children's exploratory outdoor physical exercise should be held as equally important.

You will need to persuade your senior colleagues about the value of outdoor play because chances are, they won't understand it or value it. A learning walk or a book scrutiny cannot access or compute the rich learning that happens outdoors. It lies beyond the parameter of learning in its non-progressive sense. Persuade, then invest. Invest time, budget, energy. Like our indoors provision, begin by stripping away everything. Start again. Think: what experiences am I trying to give the children out here? Most importantly, think: how can I use those experiences for the 3Ms? If my SLT comes to visit, how can this outdoor play demonstrate the kind of learning that the adult world demands? How can I, as facilitator, utilise outdoor play as another tool that feeds on children's high engagement and interpretation? Am I going to create a space that operates beyond my use or am I going to create one that exudes a richness that I can use effectively?

Taking your indoor provision and plonking it outside is not the great outdoors

I'm sorry to say but it is not. Your outdoor space should complement but it should not directly mirror the indoors. Duplo in a Tuff Spot is not outdoors provision. Your outdoor space should live and breathe – it should be a microcosm of the world beyond. Make Narnia and your children will live in Narnia.

An effective outdoor space should offer children the opportunity to take risks, to collaborate, to explore and interpret for themselves. If you're fortunate enough to have established trees in your setting, then let the children climb them. If you're worried about them falling from a great height, then come together with the children to negotiate rules and how to stay safe. If need be, tie ribbon round the tree to indicate how high they can climb, but do this in negotiation with them. Climb with them, test the branches with them, remove branches that might cause you concern, but again do it with the children. Model risk taking; use it as an opportunity to discuss staying safe and how to measure risk. Climbing trees is becoming a lost skill and yet it can be one of the richest experiences of childhood. Think about what 3Ms opportunities exist with tree climbing – label writing, lists of rules, rote counting, language extension, swinging, pulling, muscle development, negotiation skills, confidence, self-control. Many schools ban tree-climbing, but they are denying children a richness that is almost impossible to re-create any other way. As humans, we are deeply connected to trees. They hold a deep-rooted significance within our primal unconscious. They offer shelter, shade, fuel, spirituality and, of course, breathe life into our eco-system. Their sacredness should be opened to children's young minds through enabling them to interact and co-exist with them. So make the most of any tree in your outdoor space. See trees as a learning friend who will repay you again and again.

CHAPTER 14

YOUR OUTDOOR SPACE

Your outdoor space should be steeped in collaborative play. Think about creating zones within the space that can by themselves become their own little learning space. Divide it into areas within which children can focus and immerse themselves. A wide open space often lends itself to running and charging – great for short bursts but potentially trickier if you want to apply the 3Ms. I like to think that an outdoor space works best with nooks and crannies, hidey-holes where children can absorb themselves. These little crannies can also harbour children from the more physical types of play that can sometimes spill over and interfere with calmer play.

So what should a great outdoors space look like? What provision will work effectively? We've already seen that provision should not need long-term and consistent adult management. Scooters and bikes are great for physical development and do give many opportunities for Personal, Social and Emotional Development as well as mark making and mathematics, but in my experience they will often lead to disputes that run and run, and can even engender selfishness and inequality very early on. If this is the case for your cohort, then I would be tempted to store the bikes away and reconsider how you use them.

We're trying to achieve a balance of large scale and nooks. Large-scale provision could include water, sand, gravel, mud kitchens, digging pits, garden plots, obstacle courses and mature trees, if you're lucky enough to have them. Nooks are great for dens. All of the spaces should lend them-selves to open-endedness.

Whatever zones you choose to set up outside, you need to consider first how each one will be 3M-able. Almost certainly think about how children and yourself are going to be able to mark make within their play. Paper and clipboards can certainly play a role, but when the weather turns these can be less effective. Big chalkboards at child height, both vertical and horizon-tal, are more weatherproof and are worth considering in each zone.

Water

I would be inclined to include at least four water trays, surrounded by pip-ing, drainpipes, funnels, containers, sieves – in fact, any resource that enables interpretation. Big-scale water instantly creates the conditions for collaboration, but at the same time can also enable isolated play too, if not all the children want to undertake a singular exploration. Often in my own setting the children convert the water zone into a factory of some sort, with each child taking on negotiated roles for collecting, measuring, stirring, pouring, bottling and refilling. This kind of play is so rich for the 3Ms, but of course your children will bring their own experiences and interests, so yours may become something very different. On one occasion, our water zone became a cider and beer factory, and I was very happy to be desig-nated chief taster, although I did have to talk to parents at the end of the day and explain that I hadn't got the children working in a real brewing company as child labour. Like our indoor environment, you will get the richest play if you don't set up the zone for the children. Present the tools and allow them to invest their imagination.

Sand

Like the water zone, a large-scale sand area is the ideal. Big enough for ten children at least and not set up in advance, it should enable a similar level of collaboration. Natural materials, bricks both real and wooden, buckets, wheel-barrows, trowels, spades, stones, logs, small world animals and wheeled toys are all welcome additions to this zone. A large-scale sand area immediately suggests to most children that this is a space to build in.

Castles, bases, space stations, pony houses, hobbit homes, forests, the beach and even a zombie hideout have reared their heads. Negotiation skills, role playing, rule making and working to achieve a collective outcome come spilling out from this zone. And when you agree that water can come into the sand pit, then you have a killer combination.

Gravel pit

Thinking large scale again, a gravel pit is a great addition to the outdoor environment. It can have similar resources to the sand zone, but offers a different material with which to explore and connect with. It's also worth thinking about adding in pipes to this zone since gravel can behave a little like water once the right angle is perfected. Gravel lends itself to building, but as it's harder to shape, the play tends to become volcano based. Its weight is ideal for physical development, too, especially if you can set up a pulley system with buckets and piping.

Mud kitchen

Food is a natural driver for children and something that is very much within their daily experience. Being in a kitchen enables rich role-playing opportunities and who doesn't love mud and pine-cone soup? I'd recommend making the mud kitchen as large as you can, with storage areas for ingredients, a central cooking area, a food display area and a café too. I'd also think about making a mini satellite kitchen elsewhere within the outdoor space so that children can access role play without necessarily having to involve themselves in large-scale play. A little nook is ideal for this.

The mud kitchen lends itself to connecting children to the natural world if you stock it with an ever-changing array of ingredients such as pine cones, petals, sticks, stones, bark, fruit, vegetables and, of course, water and mud. Supply tools such as pans, real cutlery, teapots – in fact, anything within reason that you would find in a real kitchen. Children bring a high level of engagement to the mud kitchen. They will be desperate for you to taste their carefully prepared food and through this high engagement, you will have ample opportunity to bring the 3Ms into their play.

Digging pits

As well as getting thoroughly wet, most children also seem to revel in getting muddy – in fact, very muddy. A digging pit meets this fascination full on. Real spades, buckets, trowels, hand forks, seeds, objects to bury, bulbs, and, if you're feeling extra brave, water. Treasure hunting, bug searching, worm collecting – exploration is the key word here. Go big scale again here. Can the space accommodate ten children? Are there different levels within the area since having them will develop body strength when moving soil?

Garden plots

Growing food with children is amazing in itself as well as being great for understanding of the world and the 3Ms. It's often sensible to establish two distinct growing areas: an adult/child one and a child one. The reason to do this is so that the adult/child one can be a harbour from rogue spade digging/fruit picking/worm hunting, while the child one can be more experimental and less upsetting for all involved if someone takes a trowel to it. You can make both as big or as small as you feel appropriate – both can have the same level of importance, if you wish. The biggest challenge is growing things that come into season outside the school holidays. A glut of strawberries is no good to anyone in August. If no one on your team is green fingered, then look for parental help or grandparents who are often more than happy to potter and lend their knowledge. Ultimately, a space in which children can observe, get hands on and contribute is perfect, and you never know, you might even get them eating vegetables by the handful.

Obstacle course

One of my favourite zones involves anything to do with tyres. They're brilliant as a tool to interpret and the imagination that children bring to them never ceases to amaze me. Any obstacle course worth its salt will include planks of varying lengths and tyres of various sizes. Tractor tyres when laid on their side are the ideal height for jumping off, but are also great to hide in. Before putting them into your outdoor space, carefully drill several drainage holes in each one, being conscious not to drill through the metal wire inside many tyres, otherwise you are making a lethal hazard. Apply the same principle of not setting up. Present the resources in a pile and allow the children to bring their magic. Collaboration, rule making, assessing risk, negotiation and instructional talk will come out in abundance. And remember that if the obstacle course turns into a plane or a base or a pirate ship, then let it evolve – the resources don't have to be an obstacle course after all.

Dens

Much of the great outdoors will lend itself to communication and the bigger scale you make it, the more talk you will potentially enable. Dens, however, are the opposite. These small spaces that perhaps only fit two people in are little bubbles of warmth, safety and chat. Make these from whatever resources you wish – tent canvas, wind breaks, plastic storage boxes, pallets, fencing, trellis, branches – the idea is for children to squirrel themselves away. The best dens are empty other than seating, as long as children are able to take resources in with them. These simple communication spaces overflow with language and chat, so don't forget to make some of them just about big enough for yourself to get in so you can model and join in the conversation. Now and again it's a great exercise to move all the dens together to make a mini village with a central space not forgetting to make this as open-ended as you can.

Rules

The great outdoors offers a unique blend of exploration and connection. Both, however, need a layer of risk assessment as we've already seen when thinking about trees. It's better to assess the risk with the children directly and negotiate with them since this makes it more real and meaningful to them. Some rules need to be considered so that the maximum 3Ms opportunities can take place and it's more than appropriate to discuss this with the children so that they understand the nature of the outdoor space. Yes, we're exploring, but we're also learning, so therefore have a responsibility.

Some rules you may want to establish might well involve practical considerations, too. You will want to reduce the amount of tidying up or changing of children, so getting ground rules and expectations across early is key. Water presents many challenges with children. Negotiate which areas of the garden they can take water into and explain why some areas are to stay water-free. If the digging area becomes a swamp, can children dig and explore? If all the sand gets emptied out of the sand pit, can we make castles and does loose sand on hard surfaces make a slipping hazard? Children need to understand that resources cost money. I like sand to stay as best as it can in the sand pit area since it costs around £300–£400 to refill it. Common sense and your own beliefs in the freedoms that children should have will guide you here, but I'd urge you to think first and foremost whether you can 3M in this space now if you allow or have allowed this to happen. If seven children get soaked from head to toe, what impact will this have when it comes to the next carpet time? The 3Ms should be your driving thought in considering these outcomes.

One final thought about the great outdoors. The Norwegians have a saying that there is no bad weather, just bad clothes. Invest in all-in-ones and wellies. Avoid closing your garden space just because it's raining. Rain brings its own brand of magic. If need be, close particular areas if you feel that they present increased risk (the trees can often be slippery because of the rain, for example). Think back to your own childhood when puddles and rain catching was a delight. Use these for the positives of the 3Ms. Please don't just close the door because by doing so you close down your children.

PART 5

PARTNERS

CHAPTER 15

PARENTS

Throughout my life my parents have always wanted the best for me. But that is what struck me – how do parents know what is best? How are we instructed and guided to be the best-version-of-ourselves as parents? Where do we learn how to be a parent? I don't remember being taught at school. I don't recall my parents giving me an instruction manual. When my daughter was born, we came home from hospital with this beautiful little girl all wrapped and delicious, and my wife and I sat on the sofa, exhausted but happy, looked at each other and said at the same time, 'Now what?'

What I quickly learned was that I didn't have a clue how to be a parent, that I was unprepared and unclear on how to raise another human. I learned on the hoof and used my store of common sense to get me through. I made mistakes, I blundered in the dark, I relied on my wife's patience and understanding to guide me. Reading books didn't really help because my daughter didn't seem to be like the children these books described. She didn't sleep, cried all the time, wouldn't step on grass with her bare feet, and didn't like to be left with anyone other than her mum and dad.

Our lives got tipped upside down and I didn't have the first clue how to change that. In a nutshell, it was really hard. And yet over time I started to get a grip of myself and began to understand what being a dad really meant, that being a parent was difficult and challenging, but at the same time the most amazing thing I had ever done. Fifteen years on my daughter is an incredible young woman and I have a beautiful and funny son too, both of whom I am immensely proud of. Inside both of them I see traits of me and my wife, both the good and the not so good, but what I have tried to do is parent them by looking back at my own upbringing and deciding what elements of it I would use and those that I wouldn't. I tried to think like a child, made sure that I talked to them a lot, took them places where they could explore, and gave them simple things that would bring simple happiness.

I said earlier that parents don't give us an instruction manual, but in some ways they actually do. Unconsciously, every single interaction and word serves to define our childhoods. Children are watching and listening all the time, absorbing every little detail. Our relationships as adults, how we treat one another, the actions we take between one another, the words we say and how we say them, all begin to build our children and shape them into the persons they will one day become, which is why when you really think about it, it is surprising that more isn't done with young people as they grow up to give them some of the essential skills for parenting. Parenting seems to happen through a combination of pot luck, guesswork and hand-me-downs.

Being the best-version-of-ourselves is a mainstay of us as humans – a striving to want to be the best and make a contribution, however small it may seem. So what does the best-version-of-ourself look like when it comes to considering parenting? Is it possible to define the things that are important and will help build a child who is ultimately self-confident, respectful and able in turn to hand positive ways on to their own?

At the heart of this consideration lies the question, what is it that children themselves want or need from their parents? What do we need to give them that they are seeking? The answer is something that will cost you nothing. Simply it is time. Your child needs your time. They don't actually need the latest toy or gift, although yes, these are lovely to receive and can be an emblem of our care for them. But a gift given without time is an empty gift.

Children want you to spend time with them

Children want you to share with them, talk, sit with them and yes, play with them. And here is the crux because adults don't live in a world of time.

They live in a world of money/not-money, relationship/not-relationship, career/not-career, time/not-time and in many cases one that includes them trying to heal the damage that they feel was done to them in their own childhoods. This is a huge wall between children and their parents. Me-time for parents is something that is often craved. Time in the shed, the garden, away with the girls or boys, in the coffee shop. A friend of a friend used to tell his wife every day that his work finished at 5.30 and he'd be home for 6.15pm on the dot to be with her and their three children. And, indeed, he was home bang on as promised, but in fact his work finished at 5pm and he would park his car round the corner from the family home and sit in it reading the newspaper until 6.13pm.

At the time I was told this tale I thought it was very funny, but on reflection I think now that this is an inditement of the adult world, a selfish pursuit of me-time when his children were at home waiting for time to be spent with them. Of course, me-time is important for adults – time to reflect and relax, but this must not come at the cost of our children. Unfortunately, however, on many occasions it does.

Children want time with you. They want you to value them and listen to their language, going full circle to our discussions about Reggio Emilia and the *One Hundred Languages of Children*. I often talk to parents and say, 'You had them, now be with them.' In most cases, this is true. Parents need to wake up to their responsibilities for their own children. If they do, then at least their children have a foundation to work from. If they don't. then they are probably dooming them to live their lives within a circle that goes round and round, each generation handing mistakes and lack of opportunity on to the next.

Somehow we need to grab hold of parents and get them to rub their eyes and see the world that their children are entering. We need to show them that as parents they can at least try to change the pattern, that they can and do have an impact, and indeed they have a responsibility to ensure that this is a positive one.

So what do parents need to do?

What skills and experiences do parents need to have to be the best-version-of-themselves? We've seen that time is integral to this and if time needs to be made and it means fewer episodes of *Eastenders* or cigarettes, or in the pub or on our phones, then this has to be a price worth paying. The following list is a summary of work I've done with various parents in my own school, parents of those children who excel or find school easy. I held focus groups with them to see if I could get a sense of the whatness of quality parenting. The group was made up of mums, dads, grandparents and single parents, and the list that was compiled was very interesting indeed. Here it is in no particular order:

Eating together as a family in the same room at least twice a week.

Talking to children a lot, involving them in day-to-day chit-chat.

Singing and saying nursery rhymes.

Reading a bedtime book every night.

Asking them to choose favourite books to read.

Going to the library once a month.

Involving children in meal preparation.

Limiting screen times and electronics use.

Regular sleep times and not allowing electronics in bedrooms beyond a certain time.

Not allowing children to watch inappropriate TV programmes or games.

Being patient.

Telling children that you love them and why.

Having firm boundaries and explaining them.

Keeping to boundaries and not allowing children to negotiate.

Having the same expectations as a partner.

Not criticising children.

Seeing children as partners in a relationship.

Playing with them.

Finding out from school or nursery how you can help them.

Listening to children and giving them time to talk.

Reading this list you can see two very clear things. All of the above involve making time. None of the above cost any money. So if that is true, then the list can be achieved by every parent regardless of economic circumstance or background. Yes, the amounts of time may vary in each case, but time can still be found and if it can't, then it *needs* to be found. 'Oh, but I'm too busy. I need to do ... [insert adult world consideration]'. Well, dear reader, 'You had them, so step up and find time' – a tough message but one that needs to be said. You'll meet many parents along your way who struggle to make time. Don't be a puppy dog and simply roll over.

This is the ultimate challenge. Enabling the parents of the children we teach to see just what lies ahead of them in school, both in primary and secondary. Most parents have no real idea. School is often seen as a place to be feared based on our own previous experience or one that enables adults to be child-free so that they can get on in the adult world.

We need to reshape how education is perceived

The only way to do this is to foster truly close relationships with parents. We need to open their eyes to the journey ahead so that they can play their part in assisting their children on the way. Unfortunately, many parents either can't or don't want to. They are passing their own misery on to their children, instilling in them the belief that school is a place in which to fail.

Our current education system does little to help break this perception. It is dominated by test and measure, and has become a treadmill that requires more business acumen than pedagogy. The truth is that this can never change if parents aren't made aware of what their children have to go through. In Early Years, we can play and there is an argument that play can be extended into KS1 and KS2, but the pressures of the adult world squeeze this possibility. It creates a dry husk with little richness of child-centred thinking. Parents can change this since parents are the voters. Getting parents on board so that they can see what education really should be and what its purpose is, is what can make a difference.

And the journey starts with one parent, then two, then three, and so on. Grab the bull by the horns and get in among your parents. Inform them, enlighten them, give them the opportunity to have their voice – in a way, treat them like children. Listen to their language and guide them when necessary. Believe me, they'll need a lot of guidance.

The first thing to convince parents about is the importance of play

If you are play-based and child-centred, then so should your parents be. One successful way I've found of doing is this is to run workshops for parents. After school and perhaps repeated too, these workshops are aimed at all parents and exploring with them the various key areas that they need to understand. It's often helpful to have a register and tempt parents to attend with various rewards such as their first reading book or library card. In these workshops the aim is for the parents to come away convinced that they need to step up and help move their child forward. Workshops I have put on have included: Understanding the Importance of Play, How to Read at Home with your Child, Getting a Grip with Phonics, What Can I do at Home that will Support their Mathematical Thinking?, and Understanding the Pedagogy of Play.

If your parents don't engage or don't understand, then how can they be the best-version-of-themselves? You need to open the door for them because they often don't realise that the door exists.

I think this is really true when it comes to parents' knowledge of KS1 and KS2. They don't necessarily know what their child has to do or how to do it. They don't realise that the skills developed in the Early Years are vital for their onward journey. They have to understand that they have a role in this. For example, if they don't practise reading at home, then their child will struggle because they won't have the fluency of reading to develop their comprehension of texts. So if we know that parents aren't reading at home with their child, should we just accept this and ask another parent to come in to school and listen to them read? No, our first step must be to explore with the parent the reasons why they are not finding time to do it, explain to them the importance and then try to support them in finding the 5 minutes in the day to do it. Of course, on paper it is not always that easy, but what we are trying to do here is engender the understanding within parents that they have a role to play in their child's development in education. All too often there is a wall between parents and school, and this wall gets handed on to their children.

We need to help ourselves, however. We need to establish relationships and trust quickly. This isn't about pretending to care. It is about actually caring. If you have parents on board who understand and are on your team, the up side to this is that your life will be easier too. Your role goes beyond the traditional view of a teacher here. You are becoming a home support worker too.

Many parents simply don't know what lies ahead of their children and the following is the horror story that goes against everything I've just written about.

By the time they get to you it's often too late

A child's development from birth to the age of 3 is possibly the most important and impactful of their lives. The love, attention and nurturing they receive during this three-year phase will stay with them forever, enable them to form positive relationships, give them the language skills to communicate, foster a love of reading and words, enable their physicality and their fundamental ability to control their very selves. It will shape their perception of humanity and what it means to be alive. It is vital that these formative years are spent in a rich and fulfilling way. Everything that is modelled to them serves to shape them in small ways that forms a whole.

We know, however, that many children don't come to our setting having experienced this. They have endured three years of poor language skills, low vocabulary, little attention, possibly abuse or neglect and very limited interaction with the written word. They then come to us in our setting already behind their peers who have been nurtured and loved. The gap that the government is so keen to close is already there. Unfortunately, it is very difficult to truly close this gap. Research shows that disadvantaged children will have heard 3 million fewer words than their enriched peers. That gap is hugely significant. So again, it comes back to us as teachers. What can we do, if we know this, if we are aware of the struggle that these particular children will face? What action can we take to make a difference and make a change?

It's about resetting our vision of what our role is. Increasingly, schools are beginning to take on work with 2-year-olds, which is admirable but only if it's not about getting them into the factory early and trying to guarantee numbers for the school business manager. Involvement with children that young has to come from the heart. It needs to be centred on an endeavour to make a change, to get in among parents and begin the process of enlightening them to what they can do to be the best-version-of-themselves.

We need to be among other Early Years settings in our locality, working alongside them, finding time to visit or opening up our own setting on a weekend for parents to come and visit. Promoting quality parenting through workshops is also another angle. Essentially, we need to take on a John the Baptist role, spreading the good word and putting in efforts that lie beyond our predefined role. Again, this sounds easier said than done, but the fact remains that if we know something, if we are conscious that parenting skills are vital for 0–3-year-olds, then it is our duty to meet this challenge. Be the change that you wish to see. Don't wait for others to do it. Be the change, be the difference.

CHAPTER 16

TAs

Increasingly, the education system is questioning the role of the TA and this, combined with the ever-growing tightening of school budgets and government funding, has led to a decline in the number of TAs and support staff within our schools. Much research has been carried out to try to show that TAs have a minimal impact on learning, although it would seem that the majority of this research is adult-world driven.

There is a case, however, to argue that TAs can actually inhibit learning within our primary schools because they can unconsciously create a reliance on an adult rather than the children in question applying their own understanding or resourcefulness. You might be surprised to hear that I actually agree with this. A TA can indeed end up spoon-feeding children and inhibiting them more than helping them. The answer to this is not to remove TAs from our schools but *rather it is to reimagine them.*

The role of the TA

If you have absorbed previous chapters and are considering children's next steps in your practice, then you need to think about the role of your TA. If you are fortunate enough to have one, then how should you utilise them? More importantly, how should you perceive them as people and how can you help them become the best-version-of-themselves?

It is a sad state of affairs that as a state, we value our educational support staff so little that we pay them less than they might earn at a supermarket. Already, we ensure as a society that we hold those who work in education in low regard. When I worked in mental health, the picture was the same. Low pay, low 'value'. Plus, we also then make it hard to attract the people who might actually play an incredibly positive role in young people's lives.

Now that is not to say that there are many people working to support children who are not amazing and dedicated. They are out there, working hard and with no complaint. However, there are equally as many people who are working in our schools who are low skilled or doing the job more to fit in with family or lifestyle. We need to think bigger than this. We need to provide the conditions for our support staff to feel the passion and energy that we have. We have to accept the things that we cannot change – pay and conditions, for example – but strive to change the things that we can influence.

Ultimately you need to get your support staff on board with your play-based vision

You probably work with people who are settled in their ways, have worked in your setting for a long time, or are 'blockers' – those who are resistant to change no matter what because they may see no reason to change or who are generally negatively minded. You cannot create a positive environment or an effective play-based, child-centred pedagogy if someone you work with either can't or won't 'get' what you are trying to achieve. Your primary goal even before you begin the journey with your children is to prepare your own team for the adventure ahead.

First, it's a question of vocabulary. We've seen how altering our own label from 'teacher' to 'facilitator' helps us make a significant mind shift in the way we perceive ourselves and our own role with children. So let's do the same with our TAs. Give them exactly the same label as you. They facilitate as much as you do within the day, after all. This subtle change immediately brings them on to your level. It helps them see their role for what it truly is – as a partner and as a co-collaborator. There's no division now. You're not 'above' them. You are next to them. Yes, you are paid more and yes, you have the greater responsibility, but on a day-to-day level they are now alongside you. Mentally, it gives them more weight and puts in their minds that they are part of something. Of course, you are still in control, but we are considering the power of words here and the impact that they can have on people either positively or negatively.

Ideas

'All for love and love for all ...' – Love For All, *The Lilac Time*

This sense of unity and equality has to go beyond words, however. If in reality you treat your team as beneath you, then of course very quickly they will see it as a veneer. As we have seen already, you sometimes have to treat adults like children, so to do this listen to their language. Use the skills that you are using with your children with the adults around you. Stop, look and listen. Take on board their frustrations, their fears, their doubts. Show them that you care by giving time to discuss things that they are finding difficult or too easy.

Working with young children in particular can be emotionally draining much of the time. Your team needs you to listen, to sympathise and to give guidance. Get down to their level. Just like the children you work with, the adults will come in each day with their own 'story' and background. A compassionate ally waiting for them when they come in can make a difference between a good or a bad day.

Of course, there is a level of professionalism that requires us to put our personal adult world to one side, but how much easier this will be if our team knows that they have offloaded or chatted about their lives. You are not a social worker to them or a miracle worker and you don't have to be their Best Friend Forever, but you can have a store of warmth and a smile that can bring about positive thinking and a focus on the day.

What's incredible about this is that in a heartbeat you will also have people around you who will listen to you too, who will be there for you when you have a tough day, who sometimes will have to pull you through. You live in the adult world like it or not, and you need adults around you who are going through the same challenges and victories alongside you.

This way of working ensures that all of you are becoming the best-versions-of-yourselves. See it as a self-help cycle not born of weakness but of strength that will ultimately equip you all to enter the children's world with passion and energy, which is exactly what they need.

Now for the final shift

Again, it concerns words. Try it and see what happens for you. Take the word 'team' and replace it with 'family'. Your team is a family. It will have its ups and downs, its changes and its challenges. But family always sticks together no matter what. You succeed together, you struggle together. You laugh together and you cry together. My own 'family' has been on the journey with me for the last seven years or so and in that time we've gone through great highs in our practice, real lows at times, personal stories such as bereavement, cancer, relationship break-up, births, marriages. It becomes the human face of work, the real adult world that can't be touched by the cold hand of data or outcomes or learning walks. This is what ties us together and creates the bond that will enable a vision to be driven forward. You go hand in hand into the future, knowing that as a 'family' you are there for one another both personally and professionally. If you neglect to nurture this family feel, then you will be engaging in a struggle on a daily basis. It is vital that you create the conditions for this to happen. Make this your first goal. Nurture the adult world so that you can throw your energies into the world of the child. You'll need your 'family' every step of the way.

CHAPTER 17

THE HEADTEACHER

'Open wide the hymns you hide ...' – Things Behind the Sun, Nick Drake

If your headteacher gets Early Years and the value of play and its power to create emotional connection to learning, then go and give them a hug. If your head doesn't then read on...

When it comes to Early Years, headteachers (on the whole) are on unfamiliar ground. They are presented with an EYFS curriculum that they don't necessarily understand fully, observing practice that they don't completely comprehend and when they pay a visit on the inevitable learning walk find themselves knee-deep in little children whose playfulness will be like a foreign language. Headteachers are most comfortable with leadership, management, data and governors' meetings. They are most commonly Upper Key Stage 2 teachers who will have had little if any training or direct teaching experience of Early Years.

There is currently a crisis in headteacher recruitment. The scrutinous eye of Ofsted, unrealistic targets and teachers leaving the profession in droves has led to schools finding it difficult to recruit leaders. Over 10,000 deputies and headteachers are over 55 and a recent survey by the National Governors Association found that 43 per cent of schools found it difficult to find appropriate applicants for their leadership vacancies. What a negative picture and unfortunately it is one that gets even worse.

The growing proliferation of Multi-Academy Trusts and our obsession with measuring outcomes means that those who are the least inclined to see true child development are the ones rising to the top. Headteachers are increasingly becoming more like managers, a situation that potentially isn't helped by the need for the headship qualification NPQH being scrapped. This has opened the door to the manager-brand of school leader. These kinds of heads are interested in data, finance, measurability – what comes in and what goes out. Arguably, we have found ourselves in the perverse situation that our schools are more akin to Victorian factories, pushing children through various stages in order to achieve an outcome. I often envisage schools with tall red brick chimneys on them, spewing out thick black smoke while the children inside them are set to work and toil.

The one thing that headteachers certainly struggle with is play

Headteachers definitely understand not-play. Not-play for a headteacher is learning. It is tangible. It is measurable. It can be linked very handily to your Performance Management. That is why Early Years is being increasingly 'schoolified'. We often hear the phrase 'School Readiness' – a headteacher will see this in terms of a child's ability to 'cope' with the demands of the National Curriculum. For a headteacher it's about children being ready for Year 1 rather than Year 1 being ready for the children. It's like saying, here is what we do on our factory floor, and this is how we do it. Fit in to this system, this way of production. Increasingly, creativity and freedom within the curriculum is being sacrificed at the altar of data and performance. Do children really 'perform'? As 'factory manager' your head will want outcomes.

Please understand that I'm not being derogatory about headteachers here. They have little choice in terms of what they need to achieve each year. What they can choose, however, is the 'how'. They don't have to stick with the 'factory setting' – the default can always be rebooted and reprogrammed. If Karl Marx was to visit our modern-day schools, I'm convinced that he would be quick to recognise his theory of 'alienation' – the process whereby the worker is made to feel foreign to the products of his/her labour – being very evident. The pursuit of outcome and measurability is leading our own school leaders away from the 'workers' into a state of disconnection from the 'factory floor'. In doing so we are losing the joyfulness within education. And how do we rediscover this joy, bring it crashing back into our schools? Through play.

The 3Ms are deeply ensconced in play. It is intertwined with playfulness, child-centredness and joy. All three of these things are beyond the expectation of 'hard data', yet they are the most vital components for a truly happy and successful school. Child first, data second.

So this is where as an Early Years worker you need to take on the responsibility for being an advocate of play. It doesn't mean that you are being subversive or a trouble maker with your school, but it does mean that in any given opportunity you need to be vocal about the power of play and give your school leadership ample opportunities to see the 3Ms in action. Invite them into the classroom to come and play, take off their high heels or their tie, get on their knees and get stuck in.

The difficulty with play is that if its benefits are not understood, then there will be an unwillingness to explore using it as a tool. It's inevitable that leaders will revert to the familiar well-trodden path. Schools on the whole are now having to think more and more about specific target-driven outcomes rather than shaping children as a whole. For, after all, if the school 'fails', then leadership jobs are at stake and even the school as an entity might be at risk. Yet you now know of a way to use play to achieve these adult world outcomes while at the same time enriching children and giving them the freedom to explore and grow themselves by themselves. So if you know it, then share it.

Get the school governors into your classroom or Early Years space, seek an ally in the board of governors, talk to them, explain what you're achieving and how. Talk to parents about your practice and discuss openly with them what it is you're doing throughout the day. Parents don't necessarily understand the benefit of play-based learning. They will be bringing their own experience of school with them to the door. If you have parents who are keen to know more, then get involved in the classroom. Your role is to open eyes to the magic that the 3Ms enables.

Don't forget that play and the 3Ms don't have to stop at the Reception door

Many schools explore the use of play-based approaches in KS1 and happily some even into KS2. Promote play as a tool further through school, even if it is limited to selected subjects such as science. Be vocal about making children's experiences real and engaging, open up discussion about how collaboration, outdoor experiences and exploration can all have an important role to play further up the school.

There seems to be a perception that play is the domain of little children. How far off the mark that is. Someone decides that after a six-week break, children should enter a formal teacher-led classroom experience. Play becomes squeezed into mid-morning playtimes and golden time on a Friday afternoon while the teacher catches up on marking. This is a picture in many schools. Children can no longer express the magic they have inside them. We sweep it to one side and begin to try to fill them with 'knowledge'. Yes, the National Curriculum is dry and yes, there is a lot of content, but play and the 3Ms can still evolve to meet these needs. All too often, for example, writing becomes something that the teacher dictates in terms of content, maths and science become worksheet based, and physical activity gets crammed into PE lessons that are controlled and prescriptive.

Be vocal about this. Encourage your colleagues to consider playfulness and the 3Ms approach. It's not good enough for the answer to be 'there's too much to get through' or 'the children need to do this and that'. When you put child development at the heart of your practice, these outcomes can be achieved. Even if you are stonewalled, at least try to sow a seed. The more teachers begin to think like you, the greater chance there is that things might change. Being silent and accepting changes nothing.

CONCLUDING REMARKS

I'm now in my mid-40s. Until now, outside of my professional life, I had two ambitions. Ambition number 1 was to play professional football. I think it's pretty obvious that I've now accepted that this will never materialise even if I played in goal. The occasional Sunday morning game leaves me in a breathless heap on the floor after only 15 minutes. My body aches for days after and it takes real exertion just to walk without my thigh muscles crying out for rest. I think I can safely say that this ambition will never be realised. All that is left for me is to continue Sunday morning kickabouts that will inevitably morph into games of walking football when I tip into my 50s.

Ambition number 2, however, is still alive and kicking – and that is to form my own band. I've wanted to do this since I was 17 when my best mate Fran Brown and I wrote a song in his bedroom entitled *Don't Fear the Pooh Goose* (don't ask) and although I did join a band in my 20s, it was never as great an experience as I wanted. Now 45, I have finally begun to see my ambition become a reality. Cruyff will probably be the band that you'll never hear of outside the pages of this book, but in its own small way it is the realisation of a dream. Around two years ago, I started feeling very happy. I don't know why, but I had a continuous sense of elation and endorphin-rush. No matter what came my way, I couldn't ever seem to feel unhappy or upset. My brain didn't want to allow it. Now call it the result of a midlife crisis if you wish, but I suddenly started to hear songs in my brain, lyrics and guitar riffs, string arrangements and bass lines. I spent a year writing and forming a band to play them. I had songs in my heart and I needed to share them.

And just like me and Cruyff, you need to feel exactly the same about play. Play should make your heart sing. Don't just know it – be it. Play should be your language. The 3Ms can be your song.

Be the change that you want to see.

Strive to be the best version of yourself.

And if you truly have a song in your heart, then sing it.

THE SCALES OF WRITING SKILLS PRESENTATION

THE SCALE OF WRITING SKILLS PROGRESSION

Daily Whole Body Exercise	Daily Dough Manipulation	Daily Finger Strength Exercise	Gross Writing Movement	Letter Recognition Formation and Direction	CVC Word Writing	Phrase Writing Finger Spaces	Short Sentence Writing Full Stops	Linking Ideas	Independent Writing	Capital Letters	Spellings	Sentence Structure
Gross Motor Whole Body	Gross Motor Arms and Core	Fine Motor Control	Feeling the Flow	Patterns and Memory	Applying Segmenting	Under-standing 'word'	Understanding 'endings'	Seeing Beyond One Sentence	Applying Skills Consistently	Understanding 'beginnings'	Seeing Patterns	Extending

JOY, ENGAGEMENT AND PURPOSE

Use the Scale to move children's names from each box left to right as their next steps emerge and develop all the while ensuring that joy, engagement and purpose are at the forefront of your adult thinking.

Keep the process and outcomes as tightly knitted to a child's next steps as possible remembering to model steps further down the Scale to 'map out the journey ahead'.

FINAL WORD

It's never easy trying to bring about change, especially when you may feel like you are 'up against it'! The clamour for so-called 'school readiness' and for EY teachers to be more 'school-y' through formal approaches is one that needs to be challenged. Once you recognise the magic of children and how critical it is to embrace as a tool, then the more likely you will be to spread the word both in your school and beyond. Change for good can start with just one voice. Make that voice yours.

For further resources and to share your experiences please visit **www.can igoandplaynow.com** – let's make a difference together, Greg :)

INDEX